AF607813

Practical Realism and Moral Psychology

Jonathan Jacobs

GEORGETOWN UNIVERSITY PRESS / WASHINGTON, D.C.

Georgetown University Press, Washington, D.C. 20007

10 9 8 7 6 5 4 3 2 1 1995
THIS VOLUME IS PRINTED ON ACID-FREE OFFSET BOOKPAPER.

Library of Congress Cataloging-in-Publication Data

Jacobs, Jonathan A.
Practical realism and moral psychology / Jonathan Jacobs.
p. cm.
Includes bibliographical references.
1. Realism. 2. Self-acceptance. 3. Reasoning. 4. Friendship.
5. Respect. I. Title.
B835.J33 1995
171'.2—dc20
ISBN 0-87840-583-6 94-37060

Contents

Preface

During recent years several versions of ethical realism have been developed. Do we need another? We only need the right one, and that presented here is offered in the hope that it is the right one or could be developed into it. I discuss antirealist, quasi-realist, and realist positions with fairly equal attention. So this handling of meta-ethical questions is not just part of a debate that is internal to realism. It takes up the main meta-ethical issues that anyone interested in the subject must deal with, and supplies realist answers to them. It is not a survey of positions taken with respect to metaethical issues. It is, I hope, a contribution that might make a difference to the debates about them.

The account is realist in that I accept that moral claims are literally true or false and that their truth-values depend upon the facts. Talk of facts here is not to be interpreted in terms of anything Platonic or of any special technical notion of metaphysics. To speak of the facts is to speak of how things are. To say it's a fact that the river flooded the fields is just to say that the river flooded the fields. To say it is a fact that what he did was slander the other fellow, and it's a fact that slander is wrong, is just to say that what he did was slander him, and his slandering him was wrong. Moral claims register the ethical significance of realities, and register it realistically. Values are not an additional category of entities, but what the value situation is is a matter of the facts.

Realism, I believe, is the most successful metaethic in accounting for the locus and nature of value, for both moral properties and requirements, for the pluralism and incommensurability of values, and for the phenomenology of ethical thought. It does so in cognitivist terms and, as such, does so in a manner that acknowledges the roles of both reason and reality, but without mysterious or merely convenient ontological commitments.

Perhaps the most controversial claim in this book is that there is practical cognition, and that practical cognition is motivational. In that sense, facts are prescriptive for practical reasoners. While ethical claims are to be interpreted realistically, there would be no ethical content to the world, no ethical significance to anything, in the absence of practical reasoners.[1] It is because there is *practical* cognition that there is ethical significance, that situations and actions and characteristics ethically count for something. So, it is the facts, or how things are, that is realistically prescriptive *for* practical reasoners. A good deal of this book addresses the issue of motivation, which for realists has proved at least as problematic as the ontology of value. Mark Platts asks, "Why should it not just be a brute fact about moral facts that without any such further element [he speaks of a non-cognitive mental state] their clear perception does provide sufficient grounding for action?"[2] I'll offer an account that, although it does not settle for this being a brute fact, does not undermine the realism of value.

I call this view *practical realism*. I develop this metaethical position and go on to examine some central topics in moral psychology on the basis of it. The general character of the project is Aristotelian, though it is not exegesis of his ethical philosophy and it departs from his positions in many ways. My purpose is to explicate and illustrate how reason in its practical employment can understand the ethical significance of facts about human nature and social life. In order to fulfill this purpose, some of this work is devoted to an account of how ethical considerations are to be interpreted as realist and some to an exploration of some central topics in moral psychology in these terms, namely, self-love, friendship, and respect. These have been chosen because I believe they are among the ethically most significant relations and forms of regard that human beings have about themselves and others. Self-love is ethically significant because it is a good no one would choose to be without, and its basis is knowledge of oneself as having sound conceptions of worth and acting on them. Friendship is a good we wouldn't choose to be without, and it is ethically significant because the bases for the best kind of friendship are people's knowledge and appreciation of each other as exhibiting excellences and being productive of good. Both self-love and friendship entail knowing and loving persons because of the good they exhibit and actualize. Respect is what unifies people in a common moral world. While it need not be based upon knowledge of an individual in the ways that self-love and friendship are, it is a kind of concern for others that is owed to them as practical reasoners, as equal participants in an ethically significant world. So, the discussion of moral psychology works its way up from the individual to relations with others.

These discussions of moral psychology follow chapters that present and defend a metaethic and an associated conception of practical reason. My main claim is that practical reasoning can achieve a substantive understanding of the ethical significance of facts and that this understanding can be action-guiding. In this view, the central question of metaethics is not "How can our theoretical understanding of the world be ethically significant?" Rather, the central question is "What is a right understanding of the world by practical reason?" We *do* act with a view to good, however sound or unsound our conception of what is good or choiceworthy or worthwhile. Our acting with a view to good or under concepts of what we take to be worthwhile is an exercise of our rationality. The involvement of reason makes it action and not just motion. It is not as though we have a theoretical understanding of the world somehow engaged to something else (desire, affect, etc.) in order for reason to be practical. Nor is reason practical just because it provides an informational service to the passions or a universal form to volitions or prescriptions. One of reason's practical employments is its comprehension of facts in terms of their significance for action. It is not "pure" practical reason, Kantian a priori reason, that structures and orients ethics. Practical reason's object is the world, including human nature, and practical reason understands and judges facts in terms of conceptions of worth and good relevant to action. Practical reason's telos is to do this rightly; there are sound and endorsable comprehensions of the world by it, just as there are sound and unsound comprehensions of the world by reason's theoretical employment. And this is so even if there is no specific end intrinsic to human nature. There needn't be a best kind of life for a human being for there to be fact-based human goods, needs, and interests that give content and detail to ethical considerations. There needn't be a single, comprehensive end for the exercise of practical reason in order for there to be practical cognition, the understanding of truths for practical reason.

The introduction and first two chapters describe and support this view. They explicate its realism and the role of practical reason in understanding the ethical significance of facts and in motivating and guiding action. There isn't an additional object, the good, nor are there additional value-entities along with natural and social facts. There is a world of natural and social facts, including practical reasoners, and these facts (including facts about them as practical reasoners) are ethically significant for them because they are practical reasoners.

The Aristotelian idea that ethics is grounded in our nature as rational animals and that it is intimately bound up with an understanding of practical reason and the capacities of our psychological life has, I believe, enormous merit. I hope to show that a certain conception of human nature and practical reason is supportable and explanatorily powerful, and that people are capable of a kind of practical wisdom that a great deal of moral philosophy ignores or discounts. I would like to characterize some of the aspects of that practical wisdom and thus help to credential it philosophically.

In addition to the support and background supplied by Aristotle, I will also refer to Kant. Although the project is quite un-Kantian, both in its general thrust and in its details, I will often use Kantian claims and principles to heighten contrasts with my own view. Aristotle's thinking will direct much of the accounts of self-love and friendship, Kant's will influence the account of respect and self-respect. I will refer to Kant more than appeal to him. But his thinking is central for understanding how and why respect is so morally important, though the account of it here will involve neither his nonnaturalism nor his apriorism.

One of the constant themes in this book is that the operation of practical reason is to be interpreted in terms of its objects. In order to understand practical reason, we need to consider more than its form or logic. Considerations that constitute good reasons for a practical reasoner count as such by virtue of being part of a sound or right understanding of the world. What makes reason practical is not just that it is sometimes concerned with action rather than with understanding but that it is concerned with the action-guiding of understanding. Ethics isn't just a construction *for* something (e.g. overcoming a tendency to selfishness, securing conditions of order, instituting policies of fairness); it is also an understanding *of* something. It is about the world and rational action in it, in the sense that facts about the world and human nature are the object of practical reason.

Acknowledgments

During a leave from Colgate University in 1990, I began work on some papers that have become chapters of this book. I spent the leave in England at Cambridge, where a Life Membership at Clare Hall made me feel welcome and enabled me to enjoy the university's exceptional resources. I am very grateful to Clare Hall and to the Philosophy Faculty at the University of Cambridge.

James Ross, a teacher of mine some years ago in graduate school at the University of Pennsylvania, is to be thanked for not only teaching me philosophy but teaching me to love it. He has also taught me a great deal about friendship without ever discussing the subject. My friend John Zeis at Canisius College has been helpful and supportive for many years and in many ways. He, too, is owed special thanks. The National Endowment for the Humanities awarded me a Summer Stipend in 1993, and that support is much appreciated. The Editor of the *American Catholic Philosophical Quarterly* kindly granted me permission to use portions of my article "Friendship, Self-love and Knowledge" published in 1992. Ellen Myers, the secretary of the Philosophy and Religion Department at Colgate, typed version after version of the manuscript with a combination of skill, helpfulness, and patience that has been humbling.

During the four years that I worked on this book, I became a husband and father. Nancy, Nathan, and Daniel have not just made the world different and better for me; they have made it a different and better world.

Introduction

Practical realism depends upon a certain conception of practical reason, and that is the link between the metaethical theses and the claims about moral psychology. A good deal of post-Humean moral philosophy has been skeptical of practical reason as a capacity for ethical understanding and as a motivational capacity. This project attributes to practical reason powers of both kinds. Practical reason is the link between metaethics and moral psychology in its being the capacity by which the ethical significance of facts is understood and by which one's motives and passions can be organized by that understanding. It is because we are practical reasoners that ethical concerns are real concerns for us. And it is practical reason that enables us both to achieve sound conceptions of what it is good to do and also to do it.

When we say that this is a type of moral realism, the emphasis is not only on the ontology of moral values. Indeed, the emphasis is as much on practical reason as on ontology. The idea is that in order to account for our making moral judgments at all and to diagnose some as sound or subtle or apt, and others as unsound or unsubtle or inapt, and so forth, we need to look at both our capacities for practical reasoning and at facts about our nature and the world. If there are moral insight, moral perception, moral imagination, and moral understanding, it is not because there are special moral faculties in us, nor is it because there are special objects or facts. Good biological thought and good historical thought and political vision do not depend on special, distinct faculties, and neither does moral thought, which, like the others, is thought about the world. In calling this view realism, we are committed not to an attempt to itemize what there is but to characterize moral thinking and judgment and decision as concerned with values that are not subjective or projected onto the world. Moral claims can be mistaken, uninformed, and inaccurate as descriptions of what happened and otherwise treated as factual claims. The reasoning that supports and addresses them is full-fledged reasoning, not reasoning dependent upon emotive meanings, or prescriptions, or the lordship of the passions. And concerns about objectivity, rational endorsability, adequacy to the complexity of the phenomena, and so forth, are as much in place in moral discourse as elsewhere.

In saying these things, I am not trying to deflate the realism/antirealism debate, nor am I appealing to Wittgensteinian notions of forms of life or rules and practices that shape a social world that is the basis of objectivity. The aim is not to domesticate realism in that way. We can't claim to be realists just because in making statements we *of course* take ourselves to be referring to the world, and what else could the world be but what we are referring to? There are arguments for realism, and arguments for antirealism, and their merits cannot be wholly ascertained by noticing features of discourse that are second nature to us. In *Realism and Imagination in Ethics* Sabina Lovibond argues that on Wittgensteinian grounds there is no basis for denying truth status to the propositions of ethics just as we assign it to propositions of science. "In this sense ethics is promoted to the metaphysical status enjoyed already by the sciences."[1] And as for objectivity, there is, "materially speaking," nothing else for it to be but intersubjectivity; and assertibility is a matter of "conformity to the consensual standards of sound judgment."[2]

What is briefly described above is not the realism of practical realism. In the latter, considerations about reason, rather than language, are fundamental. Ethical claims are to be interpreted realistically because facts are objects of practical cognition and we can get them right or be mistaken. This is not Platonic reason grasping a supersensible reality, or Kantian reason constructing moral value from a priori materials; it is though full-fledged reason, not reason assimilated to linguistic practice and its associated forms of life. What is shared with Lovibond's view is that ethical claims are not to be interpreted as somehow lesser than nonethical claims in propositional significance. But the explanation will be different from the one she supplies, and it differs in its commitment to the possibility of moral claims being rationally vindicated in a manner other than by articulation of their place in a form of life. Practical reason is reason that considers the world in terms of conceptions of worth and understands the grounds for and against acts, situations, and policies of action and the place of dispositions of certain kinds in a good character and a good life. We think in terms of value, of reasons for judgment, choice, and action, and in so thinking we are thinking about the world. What we need is not to reconstruct this in noncognitivist or projectivist terms but to consider what makes for thinking well in these ways. Reflection on moral discourse is important for sorting this out, but the discourse is important for what it indicates about reason and the world. The metaphysics of morals is a subject we cannot hope to get clear about without taking seriously the role of language. Looking at language helps us on our way. But language is not the primary substance of the metaphysics of morals; it is that through which the relation of reason and its objects is expressed, and that relation and its constituents are primary.

This is why so much weight is put on a robust conception of practical reason here. Reflection on the nature of moral claims is more than reflection on rules governing the use of moral terms and more than analysis of moral concepts. And it needn't be driven by comparison with scientific or some other sort of thinking. We should start with a recognition that there is practical thought, thought concerned with good action and the justifying reasons for it, and that it is a pervasive, important part of our lives. Nor is it clear that sound ethical thought issues in elaboration of rigorously systematic theory. The kinds of things that are of moral concern are pervasive and important, but the particular forms they take and their urgency often require us to make quite context-sensitive judgments and choices with fairly fine-grained attention to the facts of the case. The fact that ethical claims are to be interpreted realistically does not imply that there is, even in principle, a formalization or codification of ethics. Ethical claims and statements can be true to the world without being part of a science of it.

This approach also explains the prescriptivity of practical reason in a non-Kantian manner. Prescriptivity, in this view, is a product of reason's practical, contentful understanding. Kant opened his *Foundations of the Metaphysics of Morals* with an emphasis on the distinction between duty and inclination. Kant was not a realist about moral considerations, but the prescriptivity of practical reason is central to his view. The distinction between duty and inclination marks for him the awareness of the prescriptivity of practical reason that even the most unsophisticated person can be aware of as a centerpiece of common moral knowledge. The distinction between the prescriptivity of moral obligation and the causal impetus of inclination is based upon

Kant's claim that reason is practical. The explication of the condition for this, namely, the postulate of freedom, is part of metaphysics and not part of common moral knowledge. But metaphysical thinking is not, according to Kant, needed in order to recognize the prescriptive claim of practical reason. The notion of value that Kant defends is nonnatural, and so too is the rational causality that makes possible the realization of that value. The present account seeks to avoid non-naturalism and certainly does not involve a distinction between fact and value, with a counterpart distinction between phenomena and noumena as a basis for it. What it does share with Kant's view is the emphasis on human beings as rational agents, as beings for whom there is a practical exercise of reason, though it will be explained as an exercise that can only be guided by factual understanding and we will see that desire has a role in it as well. Neither the ends of morally sound action nor its motive, however, can be supplied only by affect or desire or subjective interest. Those who have held that they must be so supplied have generally done so on the basis of skepticism about reason's ability to motivate or to formulate or detect an end for action, or of confidence that one or another species of antirealist naturalism or projectivism is adequate to explain both value and motivation.

A great deal of metaethical argument concerns skepticism about practical reason. Theorists such as Nagel and Donagan have articulated conceptions of practical reason that are broadly Kantian in character without dependence upon a noumenal self and an a priori law of freedom.[3] Nagel, for example, argued in *The Possibility of Altruism* that structural features of practical reason show there are ethical motivations independent of desires and also ethical principles similarly independent. This view depends upon an interpretation of the metaphysics of agency that Nagel believes best accounts for rational action, both with respect to one's own interests and with respect to promoting the interests of others. It has as a result the inescapability of ethical requirements on action, an inescapability not explicable on the basis of morally neutral desires. Donagan, too, argues that there are ethical principles that are binding for a rational agent and that they are grounded in the nature of rationality. Neither theorist is committed to noumena in their accounts. They have thus partially shifted away from certain peculiarly Kantian claims the debate over whether reason is practical while retaining the Kantian notion that the metaphysics of rational action underwrites moral principles. Other theorists, such as Mackie, Harman, and Williams, have developed approaches to ethics that in a variety of ways are loyal to Humean skepticism about practical reason, either in terms of there not being value-objects for reason or in terms of reason's alleged inability to be prescriptive for action.[4]

What lies behind or at least nearby these debates over whether reason can be practical is the issue of the interpretation of human nature. Are human beings fundamentally rational beings who have passions and appetites? Or are they fundamentally passional beings who can employ reason in the service of their passions? Can rational considerations have a kind of autonomy in the sense that they can structure and motivate action on their own, or is reason's office in action a subordinate one, waiting upon prompting and direction supplied from outside reason? Depending upon what one takes to be fundamental about human nature, there will be varying accounts of what is needed for ethics. Humeans and other antirealists don't see themselves as having to make do somehow with much more austere or less muscular resources than realists or Kantians. They deny that the resources that realists and Kantians claim are needed for ethics are indeed needed. So, many theorists whose positions might appropriately be labeled "skeptical" are not skeptical about the genuineness and importance of ethical considerations. Rather, they account for them differently than realists and Kantians because of the differences in their interpretations of human nature and human action. They don't deny the reality and significance of morality; they doubt that reason can be practical and that ethical claims are to be interpreted realistically. Blackburn, for example, says of his projectivist:

> He affirms ***all that could ever properly be meant*** by saying that there are real obligations. When the context of discussion is that of first-order commitment, he is as solid as the most virtuous moralist. It is just that the explanation of why there are obligations and the rest is not quite that of untutored common sense. It deserves to be called anti-realist because it avoids the view that when we moralize we respond to, and describe, an independent aspect of reality.[5]

Practical realism is not committed to values being an independent aspect of reality in any nonnatural way. But neither does it construe ethics as supervenient upon our passional nature in the manner of Blackburn's projectivism. Maybe his quasi-realist projectivism can retain "the grammar of moral discourse." There remains the issue of the justification of what is asserted. And this, I think, is where projectivism (quasi-realist or otherwise) comes up short. The problem is not that projectivism desolemnizes ethics, taking the "really" out of "really wrong," "really just," "really obligatory." Blackburn has shown (to some extent) that metatheorizing need not undermine first-order practice in that way. I say "to some extent" because, while it is true that antirealist theory need not change our dispositions or judgments or the conviction with which the latter are offered, it does leave questions of justification unsatisfactorily answered, either by dismissal, inattention, or a refusal to be moved by them. There is a parallel here to the Humean position that we just naturally do believe there is an external world, and reason is incompetent to justify the belief, but at the same time, that's all right, we don't need reason to justify it. If the realist insists that on projectivist grounds moralizing is merely shmoralizing and that on Humean grounds objects are shmobjects, then the antirealist counsels intellectual relaxation therapy; what we have is enough with which to do all that we undertake to do. The realist is unnecessarily concerned, just getting shmupset. But this won't do. The issue is not a matter of finding a way to get "really" back into moral claims. It is a matter of justification, of explicating how moral considerations count as determiners of practical reasoning, because they are moral considerations, not just because we have a propensity to respond, act, or be affected in certain ways.

The Aristotelianism of this account is this: It is not as though we have reason over here, grasping truths and making inferences, and desire over there, supplying ends and motivational energy, and they somehow operate together to produce action. We would not act at all, we would not be *practical* reasoners unless desire was fundamental to our nature. We are animals, and as animals we are constantly moved by and aware of needs, lacks, goals, and affective responses. We live by *doing*, by realizing ends, and aiming at things. But we are rational animals, and a rational animal is an origin of action through exercising "intellect, which aims at an end and is practical;" (*N.E.* 1139b 36). Our thinking about what to do and how to do it (when engaged in carefully and energetically) is the formation of rational desire through deliberation. It is the rational articulation of desire. It is because we are passional beings that we act for ends; it is because we are rational beings that we *aim* at ends on the basis of justifying grounds and can engage in activity for the sake of considerations we understand. We move because desire is essential to us, but as actors our motion is rational motion. Desire is, so to speak, matter informed by reason, the actualization being action.

Practical realism does not account for either ethical value or motivation wholly independently of desire. But neither does it ground value or motivation in desire independent of reason. Antirealists often argue against realism about values on the ground that it cannot explain motivation. Reason and cognition, it is claimed, are motivationally inert. But this stand depends upon what is, in this view, a mistaken decomposition of reason and desire, one that attributes too little authority to the former and too much autonomy to the latter. Both value and motivation, it will be argued, involve desire, but neither is parasitic upon it.

Only reason can be prescriptive. Desire (in the Humean sense) can move us, but not prescriptively, because prescription involves a norm or a standard of correctness. In a nonrational animal desire is a motive force, but it is not prescriptive, or at least certainly not recognized as prescriptive by the animal. In a human being, reason is prescriptive, or rather our understanding of what to do is prescriptive, in that it has the authority of justifying what is done or to be done. Desire is motive, but not prescriptive, because it has energy but not authority. For a human being there is such a thing as *correct* desire, in that desire can aim at what reason understands to be what should be done. There would be no "what should be done" without desire, since it is on account of our nature, which involves appetition, that we move. But *how* we move, for at least a great deal of our motion, is potentially under the influence and authority of reason. Cognition is ingredient in action not only insofar as we are aware of many of our desires and can have beliefs about them but also in determining what to do and how. In a practical being, an individual who is an agent, reason and desire are not separate, each obeying their own laws (as, for example, Kant held, and on account of which it is a mystery how reason can be practical in that sort of view). Desire is translated into action through reason, and reason is a cause of action through desire. The Humean and Kantian dualisms of reason and desire falsely present an analytical distinction as a real one, as if the rational bits of an action and the appetitive bits could be sorted out from each other or produce action when somehow linked together. But reasoning and desiring are not simply two different kinds of things going on in us. Thinking about what to do is an exercise of reason even though we wouldn't do it at all except for our being creatures with desires. If that were not the case, there would be no thinking of something as *good to do*. But the goodness of it is not solely or primarily a function of our desiring it. To consider *x* as good to do is the business of reason, and it is reason that makes the desire correct and the action correct. *Good* is a notion that can be used in analogical ways to explain the behavior of nonrational animals, but it is not a notion for them. It is only deployed by rational animals, and not just as a rationalizing awareness of desire.

Whereas Kant began his *Foundations* with the distinction between obligation and inclination, which he claimed everyone was aware of, Aristotle opened his *Nicomachean Ethics* with the claim that action aims at some good. Both began with important claims about practical reason that were starting points for larger accounts of human action and ethics. Something much more like Aristotle's will be defended and developed here. It is immensely plausible to understand deliberation and choice and action in teleological terms, in terms of a that-for-the-sake-of-which they are engaged in. What the agent takes to be good may not be really good, and one may be in error, self-deceived, or otherwise misguided. But the notion that paradigmatically human activities such as deliberation and choice aim at realizing or obtaining some good is a starting point we should remain explanatorily tethered to. Moreover, these activities paradigmatically involve reason, even if it is uninformed or fails in some way. Aiming at a good entails having some conception of it, some understanding of the point of the action and its worth. And these conceptions can be informed and accurate or not. There is something for reason to be correct or wrong about in its practical exercise. If there were not, desires and passions would still be important in our lives, but ethics would not be. There would not be rationally endorsable norms and criteria with which to judge claims about what to do, or conceptions of good. Reason is practical in that one crucial type of human motion, that toward a good conceptually understood, is rational motion.

Here the skeptic might insist that important questions have been begged. Why concede that reason is practical if in the explanation of action it can be assigned a role that is basically instrumental and the end and motive of action can be explained with reference to considerations not traceable to reason? How can reason be both cognitive and practical? That's one way to formulate the issue. Another way, however, is to notice how thoroughly reason is implicated in action, in terms of supplying a conception of what is choice worthy and thus supplying motivational impetus to do it. One of our aims will be to show that a basically Aristotelian starting point, one that the skeptic rejects because of its affiliated notions about the functions of reason, is to be retained and elaborated. When Aristotle holds that action aims at some good and that the rational part of the soul can understand what it is good to do, he is in effect arguing that for a human being the choiceworthy is an object of a kind of understanding that is prescriptive for action. Reason has a causal role in action insofar as it can be employed to assess ends of action, assess them in terms of understanding, and orient the passions and appetites to conform with that understanding.

A more Humean line would be that it just makes no sense to attribute causality to reason except in terms of its aiding to bring about the object of desire. It can articulate desire or sentiment, elevate a passion into a conception of what to do; but both the content of what to do and the motivational energy are passional. Reason cannot autonomously achieve a conception of good or move us to act on it. This sort of approach allegedly has the advantages of disallowing excessive claims on behalf of reason and of fitting well with naturalistic claims that are philosophically popular. We only bring value and morality into the world because of our passional natures, and that's all we need in order to do so. The claims of reason are always an elaboration and extension of something that doesn't originate with reason.

On the other hand, it would be a mistake to attribute to the Humean view all the resources of articulation, argument, validation of claims, and so forth, that are part of moralizing while claiming that reason is, all the way through, playing a supporting role and in the service of something else. Hume's view isn't emotivism, and in contrast to twentieth-century emotivists, Hume was more a naturalist than an ally of them. But if we want to credit ethical argument and talk of ethical validity and invalidity and, for example, the acceptability of some claims and the unplausibility of others, then we are borrowing a great deal from cognitivism and to some extent simulating it, but claiming that the virtual reality is all the reality that is needed.

But the claims that a desire is right, or a response is appropriate, or an ethical description is apt or illuminating—and all the sorts of disputes and dialectical exploration that make sense relative to such claims—are more than expressivist stances or the working out of them.

Expressivist stances could not even be mistaken for cognitivist claims unless they took the form of statements and were elaborated into norms and criteria and critical responses figuring in argument and deliberation. That is, they have to be worked up by reason into a view of things and not just function expressively. Once worked up, they are susceptible of rational criticism, of being judged for adequacy, consistency, coherence, applicability, and so on. The point is that their prescriptivity for reasoning creatures only gets going once they are assimilated by reason and turned into conceptions, rather than just remaining propensities or symptoms of sensibility or appetite. Blackburn's quasi-realism is, in a sense, an acknowledgment of this, a way of retaining the form of cognitivism while claiming that realism is no more than an ontological trapping that can be done without. But in order for us to be cognitivists and realists about ethics, we do not have to deny the naturalistic bases and relevance of desire, sensibility, and conative stances. Practical realism is certainly not a theory of "pure" practical reason. Reason is not practical in utter detachment from desire or the passions, but they are a basis for claims and convictions and judgments only insofar as they are objects of reason. Practical reason is not just passion at work in a human being; it is reason at work in a being with appetites and feelings. Thinking in terms of good and choiceworthiness is real thinking; it is a cognitive business and the office of reason.

The concern of ethical thought, in this approach, is to clarify how our nature is the basis of considerations of good. Ethics is not primarily concerned with articulating and justifying rules that form a system of obligations constraining the activities of self-interested individuals. Nor is it primarily concerned with what requirements there are, given that one desires to live in civil society or render one's volitional prescriptions consistent and livable. Rather, it is concerned with how normative considerations for practical reason are grounded in what we are and in our capacities for action. So, the aim of this type of ethical inquiry is not to take agents' interests and concerns and find a way to moralize them. There isn't, *first*, practical reasoning, and then a system of requirements it can be engaged to. Ethics is not so much about what one is obligated to do, given that there are other people in the world. It is about what makes for good activity, given that there are considerations of intrinsic value for practical reasoners. Reason does not simply report what is good, nor does it merely aid in pursuing goods consequent upon passion or construct a good or goods. It organizes and informs our thinking in terms of what is worthwhile in action and enables us, through its prescriptive comprehension, to direct action. What is ethically good is really good, given what we really are (including our passions and appetites) and what the world is really like, and we are able to act well because we can motivationally respond to an understanding of it. The notion of good action is a success notion, and success here involves answering to understanding that is prescriptive for a being with certain sorts of desires and sensibility. It is reason that enables us to formulate conceptions of need and interest, and it is reason that can inform and articulate passion into conceptions of what is worth doing and what are appropriate responses and attitudes.

In addition to the cognitive and prescriptive capacities this account attributes to us as practical reasoners, it also maintains that a distinctive kind of pleasure is caused by the right exercise of practical reason. Reason, then, has a twofold practical causality. On the one hand, it is prescriptive in its comprehension of what facts ethically count for; on the other, its exercise causes a uniquely rich and stable type of enjoyment. Reason can tell us what is ethically good to do, and we can enjoy acting well. The causality of practical reason is itself enjoyable, and not simply one pleasure among others. For Aristotle, activity in conformity with virtue (where this includes the mature individual's practical wisdom) is desirable in itself as the pleasure of a well-ordered soul. The virtues enable one to successfully exercise and realize one's nature as a rational animal, and this success, this excellence, of human nature is something one loves. This is one way in which the metaphysics of morals and moral psychology are intimately linked for Aristotle. Excellent activity of the soul depends in part upon the activity being guided by practical reason, and practical reason has as its object factual considerations of human good.

Indeed, according to Aristotle pleasure is that by which "the soul as a whole is consciously brought into its normal state of being" (*Rhetoric* 1370a 1-2). Exercising the ethical virtues is pleasing because it is a realization of real human good, and it is normal for a rational being to be pleased by what is its appropriate excellence. Realized human excellence may not be typical; certainly perfect virtue is not. But it is normal in the sense that it is the realized norm of human nature. Excellence in activity has enjoyment of it as a natural accompaniment. Aristotle's account of pleasure is not fully worked out, and what there is of it is not as clear as we would like. Still, it is based on some insights that this account will rely on and develop. Rational activities are pleasurable because they actualize the good of the being who engages in them. One general way in which this notion will figure here is that it will be argued that a right understanding of what is good in action is pleasurable in its action-guiding employment. This is not a pleasure of the intellect, it is a pleasure of a passional, appetitive being whose passions and appetites are cognitively informed or organized. This sort of pleasure is not good feeling, like the feeling of slaking a thirst or seeing one's team win. It is appreciation and affirmation; appreciation of action as warranted and affirmation of the value involved. There will be much more on this later.

For Kant, the pleasure of well-ordered practical reason is explained quite differently, but he, too, holds that good activity is the cause of a distinctive type of enjoyment, a moral feeling. Good activity is not a part of happiness but a condition of worthiness for it. "So far as I am conscious of freedom in obeying my moral maxims, it is the exclusive source of an unchanging contentment necessarily connected with it and resting on no particular feeling."[6] This kind of satisfaction has to do exclusively with freedom, with the activity of practical reason unconditioned by anything in empirical psychology. The pleasure has to do with the operation of the will in accordance with its own law, for the sake of the law. Beck comments:

> In moral action we find a satisfaction in the experience in our own autonomous spontaneity and that this is the positive element in respect as the moral feeling. Man is humiliated by his vision of the law, before whose majesty even the boldest sinner trembles . . . but he is elevated in his consciousness that this humiliation is the mark of his higher vocation, for it is humiliation of himself by himself, of his heteronomous natural being by his autonomous intelligible being.[7]

This higher vocation is a source of enjoyment, satisfaction with one's own autonomy. Respect for the law is a cause of satisfaction in our activity of self-legislation. In Aristotle's theory the pleasure concomitant with virtue is not a matter of subordination of inclination and feeling to a moral law but is caused by the individual organizing his or her soul and activities in a way such that passion is coordinated with an understanding of what is good. But Kant and Aristotle both hold that well-ordered practical rationality yields a distinctive and important kind of enjoyment. What is particularly pertinent about this for our discussion is that it is the causality of reason that produces this enjoyment, the causality of reason either engaged to the right objects (in Aristotle's case) or following its own law (in Kant's case). Aristotle's conception of the pleasure natural to human excellence is closer to that in our discussion. When our desires are in agreement with reason in a stable manner and we act from dispositions ordered in that way, we enjoy doing so. This is not a matter of sensing or feeling but of appreciating our activity in the very engagement in it.

One of the main claims in the chapters on self-love, friendship, and respect is that when these are normatively grounded in the right ways, they yield this distinctive pleasure. When they are shaped by an understanding of normative considerations, the activities that partially constitute them contribute in a significant way to agents' well-being by being productive of pleasure. When the causality of practical reason is well ordered, part of the good it realizes is the enjoyment that gives one a reason to continue to exercise its causality in that manner.

The selection of self-love, friendship, and respect as the moral psychological topics is based on their being matters of basic human concern because of how they figure in our living good lives. It is very difficult to live well without them. Also, they are apt as topics for illustrating the metaethical claims developed in chapter 1. In that chapter an explanation of the objects and prescriptivity of practical reason will be sketched out. That will be the groundwork for developing in some detail the ethical dimensions of the specific topics that are taken up in chapters 2 through 6. In the conclusion we will take up the issue of how ethical practical reasoning is distinguished from nonethical employments of it. This is important because I hold that practical reasoning generally is to be interpreted realistically, so what makes for distinctively ethical practical reasoning needs to be made clear.

Self-love and friendship are kinds of concern for and appreciation of others and ourselves in virtue of their being loci of ethically good activity. At least in their primary sense, that is what they are. We rightly love others as friends and rightly love ourselves when we are worthy of good because we are productive of it. That, anyway, is what I shall argue. Friendship and self-love involve a kind of appreciation of persons and an active (not merely affective) concern for them based upon knowledge of them as good individuals or at least as individuals striving to be good. Respect is a kind of regard for persons based upon their being practical reasoners capable of rational self-determination.

Respect does not require knowledge of the individual in the same way as friendship and self-love, but they all center on human beings as practical reasoners. Because people are practical reasoners, a certain kind of respect is owed to them. Friendship and self-love are normatively based more upon what people do, while respect is normatively based upon what people are. All are grounded in considerations about the nature and exercise of practical reason. Two of the topics have to do with ethical relations based upon knowledge of the individual, and the other has to do with recognition of the nature of the individual.

Friendship, as I have indicated, has mainly to do with concern for another's good. This does not mean that only friends are concerned for each other's good. People can be, and hopefully are, concerned for the good of others in general. But friendship is a direct concern, based upon personal knowledge in a way that a more general kind of concern is not. Respect is more the sort of regard that is owed to someone as a practical reasoner. Kant, in the *Doctrine of Virtue,* writes:

> But man regarded as a *person*—that is, as the subject of morally practical reason—is exalted above any price; for as such (*homo noumenon*) he is not to be valued as a mere means to the ends of others or even to his own ends, but as an end in himself. He possesses, in other words, a *dignity* (an absolute inner worth) by which he exacts *respect* for himself from all other rational beings in the world: he can measure himself with every other being of this kind and value himself on a footing of equality with them.[8]

For Kant, that persons are rational agents constituted a fixed, unrevisable ground for a certain kind of respect owed to them. This is respect owed to rational personality as such, not on account of any of its particular accomplishments, ends, or activities. At the core of this is the autonomy of rational agents. It is because persons are capable of action produced by self-imposed necessity, because persons are capable of acting on the basis of the conception of laws they legislate for themselves that they are never to be treated merely as means. This respect is not a feeling of concern. It is a rational requirement on proper acknowledgment of the reality of persons. I will argue that there are objective grounds for respecting persons and that we can preserve the distinctiveness and significance of respect without endorsing a Kantian theory of practical reason.

Some theories do not give a central place to respect for persons. But it merits a central place. It is rationality that makes morality possible for human beings, makes us agents acting under concepts and capable of evaluative judgment and of some authority over our motives and passions and, as such, responsible agents. What the notion of respect captures and expresses is the significance of practical reasoners as ethical agents and thus as beings who are no one's mere instruments and no one of whom is, in its primary nature, more worthy of respect than any other. Respect is a relation between people that rationally unifies them in a moral world through acknowledgment of what kind of beings they are. In respecting others we appreciate their reality as practical reasoners and responsible agents and engage with them in a common moral world. In respecting ourselves we take ourselves seriously as agents aspiring to achieve and act on a right practical understanding of the world. Respect is that form of regard and concern through which we credit the significance of practical cognition and action and their contribution to the character of the human world.

By examining relations between ourselves and others based upon knowledge of them as individuals (self-love and friendship) and based upon regard for them as rational agents (respect), we can supply a focus for some of the most important issues in moral psychology and also better understand ethical attitudes and relations. How we regard ourselves and others and the ways in which we appreciate and value ourselves and others are fundamental exercises of practical reason. They are both causes and effects of the degree to which we have practical wisdom. This latter is learned and exercised in our relations with ourselves and with others. It is not something acquired outside of the business of living and then applied in it. This, too, is a place where there is particular strength in Aristotle's account. He was not primarily concerned with how we use words or with formalizing criteria for ethical judgment or decision making. He was more concerned with showing how character and understanding, emotion and desire actually figure in how we come to be the sorts of people we are; he was interested in the existence of general considerations about human nature, knowledge of which enables us to order our character and action to what really is good for us.

The point of starting with metaethical considerations is to lay a groundwork for explaining how practical reason's understanding of its objects is crucial to explicating these topics in moral psychology. This is not a project in normative ethics if that means the presentation of a moral theory, a theory of what are moral obligations, prohibitions, and permissions. It is not a project concerned with certain ethical problems (such as truth telling, justice, punishment, and so forth). Its aim is to characterize adequately a realist metaethic and the role of practical reason in it in order to explore some topics in moral psychology that matter in everyone's lives.

CHAPTER 1

Where in the World Is Ethical Value?

The first project is to characterize and defend what I call *practical realism*. This is a realist metaethic in that it takes realistically interpreted facts to be ethically significant, to be ethical considerations. It is practical in that it explains prescriptivity in terms of the understanding of facts by practical reason.

Moral realism has been criticized and rejected in a number of ways and on a number of grounds, ontological, epistemological, and semantic. J. L. Mackie, a critic of moral realism on all these grounds argues that "ordinary moral judgments include a claim to objectivity, an assumption that there are objective values"[1] but holds that this assumption is false. So, even someone willing to allow that people typically think moral judgments are realist finds multiple reasons to deny this. Practical realism is not primarily intended to protect "ordinary moral judgments." I am not sure Mackie is right or wrong about "ordinary moral judgments." Just as his metaethical critique is not grounded in commonsense views but is a philosophical account, so is this defense of realism. And it is intended to credential realism on ontological, epistemological and semantic grounds.

While practical realism holds that factual considerations are morally significant for practical reason, some advocates of realism might suspect that it is not realist enough. They might hold that, for it to be genuine realism, reason must be left out, in the sense that the facts are intrinsically prescriptive. That is, they might hold that realism must be of the form that Mackie rejects, a form according to which values are "entities or qualities or relations"[2] and "would have to be intrinsically action-guiding and motivating."[3] Moral realism can, however, include a role for practical reasoning. Values are not projected; they are not essentially a matter of affect or sensibility or what people's desires happen to be. Factual considerations have ethical weight because there are practical reasoners. Reason's role with respect to action is to understand facts as considerations for doing (or not doing) something. Values are not additional entities, and they do not need to be in order to be interpreted realistically. Indeed, if they were, then it would be deeply problematic, perhaps mysterious, how they could be action-guiding.

According to practical realism, reason's practical employment is to understand the world (facts, circumstances, situations, etc.) in terms of its significance for action; that is to say, practical reason is a capacity for action-guiding understanding. Aristotle held that "intellect itself, however, moves nothing, but only the intellect which aims at an end and is practical" (*N.E.*, 1139b 1–3). This is not incompatible with moral realism just because the object of thought on its own does not move us. It is a kind of realism. What is good with respect to ethics, what is intrinsically good in action, what is ethically required is an object of cognition. One of reason's practical functions is valuational understanding, and this is how reason is both cognitive and action-guiding. Part of being rational beings is our ability to respond motivationally to this understanding. As already indicated, the realism defended here does not inherit Aristotle's specific account of the teleology, the *ergon* of human nature. But the theories of value and moral motivation are descendants of it.

To credential practical realism, it has to be explained, on the one hand, how practical realism is not just like other realisms and why it is to be preferred. So we will discuss supervenience theories, which I take to be its main realist competitors, and distinguish practical realism from them. On the other hand, it must be shown why practical realism is to be preferred to positions such as Wiggins' or to Blackburn's quasi-realism, and why it is not an ethical counterpart to Putnam's internal realism. Each of these philosophers claims to identify a variety of defects in realism but, at the same time, recognizes certain of its merits and seeks to represent them in his respective position. It will be argued here that a more robust version of realism than the ones countenanced by Wiggins and Putnam can and should be defended, and that Blackburn's quasi-realism does not successfully retain the merits of realism as it purports. Putnam does not present internal realism as a metaethic. But because practical realism gives an important role to reason, not just as a detector of value-entities, it might be thought a near cousin of internal realism. But it is not. We'll see why later in the chapter.

The main claims of practical realism are that

(i) facts (realistically interpreted) are ethically significant for practical reasoners;
(ii) practical reasoners can understand the ethical significance of facts and guide action (be motivated) by that understanding;
(iii) moral values are not an additional set of entities or properties;
(iv) moral values do not supervene on nonmoral facts and properties independently of practical reasoners;
(v) moral claims have literal truth-values and are descriptive.

Claim (iv) is probably the most suspicious to realists. Why claim to be interpreting values realistically if they are in some way dependent upon reasoners? The "dependence," though, does not weaken the realism of the position. Practical realism maintains both that moral claims are literally true or false (realism about truth values) and that the determination of their truth-values turns on whether they assert what is so according to practical cognition. For it to be cognition, there must be truth; and there is practical truth. For it to be practical, it must be concerned (broadly) with what it is good to do. That it is part of the account that desire can be in agreement with understanding hardly renders less realist what is understood. It is also part of this view that the ordering of passions and desires in a certain way, engaged to the right objects, so to speak, is necessary for practical cognition. But neither does this thin out or shrink realism. Rather, it is an acknowledgment that we come to understand practical truth through a process of moral education. Still, what is understood, what is cognized is to be interpreted realistically. It is not necessary to leave the agent out of the picture for it to be a realist picture. It is necessary to include the agent realistically.

Reason, then, is practical, but it is not practical in the way Kant held. Reason has a practical teleology, and it actualizes good through informing and organizing desire. Or, rather, *we* are practical beings because our reason is a capacity that enables us to do this. One fundamental employment of reason is thinking about what to do. Practical reasoning can ratify ends, endorse them as right, and formulate permissible means to realize them. Our conceptions of what is worth doing are not simply desire-driven, if that means that they have their sources in desire independent of understanding. It is because we have desires that we are moved to act at all. But the desires can be rational desires, informed by valuational understanding.

Practical realism is located in the disputed territory bordered on one side by Platonism and on the other by emotivist and projectivist antirealisms. In this disputed territory there are battles over the extent to which ethical claims are subjective or objective, and also battles over whether they are naturalistic. We need to discuss these battles.

In the debate over whether ethical judgment is objective or subjective, the line distinguishing the two is often drawn in the wrong place. Ethics is about subjectivity in its concern with *human* needs and interests and sensibility. Ethical theorizing that did not centrally concern features of human psychology, including responses, affect, and attitudes, would not have the bearing on actual human life that it needs to have. On the other hand, ethical judgment and even ethical response are not detached from reason, are not expressions or exhibitions of affect with no admixture of perception, discrimination, and knowledge. Attitudes and responses, the emotions and passions are intentional, and there is rationally assessable content to them. Disordered sensibility includes, and sometimes simply is, a kind of failure of judgment or is, at least, a symptom of incomplete, biased, or failed understanding.[4] Our responses and the feelings that move us to appreciate a situation in a certain way can be symptomatic of a lack of understanding.

What kind of explanation could projectivism offer of disordered sensibility? I do not mean what kind of explanation could it offer of how it got that way but of what it is to be disordered. This cannot be explained except in terms of the realities it is a sensibility for, and once we bring those in, we cannot describe it except in cognitivist terms. A disordered sensibility inappropriately responds to ethical significance. McDowell remarks:

> Now projectivism can of course perfectly well accommodate the idea of assessing one's processing mechanism. But it pictures the mechanism as something that one can contemplate as an object in itself . . . at any rate one is supposed to be able to step back from any naively realistic acceptance of the values that the first-level employment of the mechanism has one attribute to items in the world. How, then, are we to understand this pictured availability of the processing mechanism as an object for contemplation, separated off from the world of value?[5]

It is difficult to see how an account that assesses the projectivist processing mechanism could avoid reference to the value-realities that projectivism denies. It is not just causal properties of reality that explain the well-ordering or ill-ordering of sensibility. And neither is it something wholly internal to the sensibility. It is what the sensibility, functioning as part of the cognitive life of a practical reasoner, recognizes and appreciates about the realities. A disordered sensibility conceptualizes and appreciates features and facts wrongly: it is not just a matter of causal mechanisms not working properly. If the business of understanding these defects is a moral business and not a matter of causal mechanisms or processes, it involves rationally assessing sensitivity to features of reality. Restoring moral sight to the morally blind is not a matter of getting them to shed light on things by projection but of getting them to see what is there and to conceptualize it properly. For example, we might counsel someone in the following way: "You're looking at this all wrong. What you want is revenge, but for one thing, there isn't anything you can do to hurt them, and more importantly, revenge is not what you should be seeking. What you need to do is think about what will help you rather than what you can do to hurt them just so that you will feel better." In remarks like these we are talking about someone's feelings, but we are appealing to their reason, and appealing to it in a way meant to modify their feelings and motives. We are urging a rethinking that reinterprets the facts and has, as a consequence, a revision of passion and what the individual takes to be good. The kind of sensibility that is morally relevant is paradigmatically undetached from reason, and this sensibility does not constitute its objects. They are to be understood in order that the sensibility be ethically sound. If this is correct, then a subjective/objective distinction for ethics that is made out in terms of "Are values objects in the world or are values a matter of the passions?" is fundamentally misguided.

Practical realism is intended to register the inseparability of the anthropocentrism of ethics, its subjective and objective dimensions, the role of cognition and the associated indices of soundness of judgment, reasoning, and discrimination. Getting clear about the objectivity and subjectivity of ethics is not a matter of locating value in the passions or in the world. Ethics is about us, and we are subjects, but cognitive subjects whose sensibility and motives can be informed and guided by understanding.

It might be argued that practical realism is misnamed and that it cannot be distinguished from projectivism. This objection is grounded in the claim that since practical realism takes facts to matter *for* practical reasoners, it is in this respect really just a species of projectivism. But this is a mistake. The present view is no more a species of projectivism than Aristotle's ethical view is, and it is like it in an important respect. Unlike projectivism, both claim that there is such a thing as a right understanding of the normative significance of facts, and both deny that this is a matter of "gilding and staining" facts by subjective projection. Aristotle is a realist in that, while he denies Platonism, he does argue that what is good for human beings is not consequent upon what human desires and sensibility happen to be, though it does depend upon what counts as right desire and passion in conformity with what reason asserts to be good. This is much the same as the claim that there is such a thing as sound appreciation of the normative significance of facts. The position differs from Aristotle's in not tying the notion of good to an intrinsic end and distinctive function of human nature that uniquely ground a best kind of life.

In his critique of theories of well-being as foundations for ethics, Bernard Williams writes:

> Even if we leave the door open to a psychology that might go some way in the Aristotelian direction, it is hard to believe that an account of human nature—if it is not already an ethical theory itself—will adequately determine one kind of ethical life as against others. Aristotle saw a certain kind of ethical, cultural, and indeed political life as a harmonious culmination of human potentialities, recoverable from an absolute understanding of nature. We have no reason to believe in that.[6]

It may be that our understanding of nature does not supply premises for conclusions about the best life, certainly not for conclusions couched in the idiom of a specific human function. Nonetheless human nature and social life may be ethically significant insofar as they supply objective considerations of human good, need, and interest. Even if there are incommensurabilities and questions that do not admit of answers in terms of this or that fact of the matter, objective reasons for choice and action can be grounded in factual considerations about human nature.[7] What are good dispositions is not a matter of sensibility unguided by understanding. And while good dispositions may not fit into a harmonious, uniquely best life, there are objective considerations of value that can both orient and justify them. In any case, while it is not wrong to say that Aristotle's conception of ethics was intended to be "recoverable from an absolute understanding of nature," it was in part recoverable from an understanding of it by practical reason and plainly not intended to be straightforwardly derivable from a scientific theory of human nature.

This is important, because seeing the issue of realism and objectivity in terms of practical reason helps to clarify how the issue of ethical value is already an issue for rationality that is concerned with action and, in at least a very general sense, aims at some good. That is, practical reason is reason that can consider facts in terms of their authority as reasons for action. It is important not to personify this notion of authority or build irresistible prescriptivity into it. Facts can not make us do anything or command practical reason to aim at this or that, or this rather than that. But reflection on what it is to be a human actor, to be an origin of action, and to direct activity under concepts and by deliberation reveals that it is part of our being human for reason to be practical. One can redescribe this in the vocabulary of one or another account of causality and thereby reassign motivational efficacy to the passions. But one will still need to explain what makes certain passions worth acting on, certain ends of action choiceworthy, and certain motives to action ethically sound. And these explanations, whether they explicitly disavow it or not, will themselves reflect judgments of practical reason.

Projectivism has an initial plausibility in nonethical matters such as aesthetic judgment and humor. It is often held that ethical judgment is analogous to these and thus is to be interpreted nonrealistically. Let us grant that projectivism works for these sorts of nonethical matters. Even if it does, ethics is hardly analogous to them. Ethical thought and argument are concerned with getting something right, and rightness here is not a result of sensibility illuminating the world in a certain way. Indeed, in the ethical context the rightness of sensibility is explained by its agreement with what reason understands. Practical cognition is prescriptive, but its prescriptivity is not derivative from something nonrational, a kind of conative energy or valuational feeling directed onto the world. Its prescriptivity is intrinsic to the cognition in that practical cognition is thought concerned with reasons for action and finds these reasons in our consideration of the world. In any case, projectivists often seem unmoved by the difficulties of the notion of projection. In some ways it is no more clear than intuition, except that in the case of projection the mystery runs forth instead of back. Projectivists want to explain rightness of judgment in terms of norms and criteria internal to a practice or kind of discourse, denying that features of what is judged are cognitively determinative of the norms and criteria. We attribute depravity to someone on the basis of our responses and can point to features of the person that justify the judgment, according to the projectivist. But that there is such a notion at all is essentially dependent upon responses or attitudes, which are not themselves cognitively informed. We do not respond to the person that way because they are depraved, but they are depraved because of our response. Projectivists may wish to deny this, but it is not clear that the denial holds up. According to realism, the person's depravity is determined by facts about that person and our judgment is a discernment of those facts. If it is not and is, instead, internal to our norms and criteria, then it is not a cognitive matter at bottom to judge them depraved.

This is not to say there are no types of projectivist judgment. The judgment that a newspaper is easy to read because the news is on the front pages and the comics and food section inside is a projection of ease. The judgment that it is not easy to read because the lines of print are spaced in random and uneven ways is either not projectivist at all or is so in a quite different way. Someone's having a virtue is a matter of that person having certain characteristics that cognitively justify the belief that that individual is virtuous. We respond to the reality with a judgment the truth-value of which is determined by features of the reality. If we refer to a car as "that damned thing" because it is broken down again, that is projection. Its being broken down again is not a matter of projection.

Ethical norms and criteria are credentialed by facts, or at least can be. There is cognitive articulation that is directive and justificatory with respect to sensibility. Loathing the car and loathing the depraved person may feel quite similar, but one is projectivist loathing and the other is not. Justification in ethics is a cognitive business insofar as it is not causally consequent to stances, attitudes, and responses that are independent of rational warrant. If one does not judge Hitler to be depraved, this is indicative of cognitive error or misunderstanding and not just a matter internal to norms with a noncognitive base.[8] Projection is not just one thing, and there are several kinds. But it is not what makes for ethical value. Projectivism as such is not an error;

it is the unchecked spreading of it, its deployment here, there, and everywhere that leads to trouble.

In some contexts it is not only not a good explanation, it is not even a plausible candidate for providing one. But its candidacy is popular because it works so well in other areas. There are too many ways in which the mind might be said to spread itself upon its objects when we are considering ethics. Any set of ethical beliefs and practices could be taken to be projectively valid provided someone regarded it as second nature to see things that way. "Well," the projectivist might say, "that's quite unfair. Realism involves the specious detection of a kind of fact, property, or entity. Projection, on the other hand, is the honest realization of attribution that is not confused with detection." Projection may be honest in that way, but for metaethics we are also concerned with whether it is true. Later in this chapter we will take up this matter in more detail. Even if one still stands by projectivism for things like aesthetics and humor (and the more thought we give to these, the more projectivism contracts), examples from all variety of practical thinking and projects make the analogy of projectivist cases to ethical cases more and more remote.

NATURALISM AND SUPERVENIENCE

Is practical realism a naturalistic metaethic? There are naturalistic realisms (Brink's, for example) and naturalistic antirealisms (Blackburn's, for example), and they involve competing interpretations of naturalism. It is a heading under which philosophers as remote from each other as Hume and Aristotle can be made to fit. Hume is an ethical naturalist insofar as his account of moral value and moral motivation is based on claims about human sensibility, desire, and propensities. Aristotle is an ethical naturalist in the sense that ethical good is human good; it is not a construct of a priori reason, and it is not a transcendent object or reality. Additionally, moral motivation is explicated in terms of features of human character. What Aristotle includes as constituents of human nature Hume would reject as metaphysical; but it is not clear that Hume's naturalism is somehow more legitimate or more faithful to the "true spirit" of naturalism. For Hume there is no rational assertion of the existence of external objects, the natural world. But he is a naturalist about ethics in the sense that he does not analyze moral predicates as merely emotive, and he gives a recognizably projectivist account of ethical claims. It is human sensibility that shapes value and value judgment, and human sensibility is naturalistic. So this is noncognitivist naturalism. Aristotle's naturalism and that of practical realism are cognitivist.

A good deal of recent metaethical debate concerns supervenience. Accounts of values as supervening have been developed by a number of realists. This approach has seemed a way to retain cognitivism without straying from naturalism. According to some of these accounts, values are not logically or semantically decomposable into the nonmoral, but they are necessarily connected to nonmoral facts and properties. This is a way of defending values from falling victim to Mackie's charge of "queerness." He argued that "if there were objective values, then they would be entities or qualities or relations of a very strange sort, utterly different from anything else in the universe. Correspondingly, if we were aware of them, it would have to be by some special faculty of moral perception or intuition, utterly different from our ordinary ways of knowing everything else."[9]

Supervenience has been a route chosen by many realists who wish to avoid commitments to exotic entities or properties, on the one hand, and skepticism, subjectivism, or Kantian constructivism, on the other. Naturalistic versions of realism purport to escape Mackie's charge of queerness by explicating how values supervene on natural and social facts and need no special faculties of cognition or perception in order to be recognized and understood. David Brink, who has developed a view of this type in his *Moral Realism and the Foundations of Ethics*, writes:

> According to the naturalist, moral facts and properties both weakly and strongly supervene on natural facts and properties. Moral facts and properties strongly supervene on natural facts and properties because some sets of natural properties necessitate certain sets of moral properties. Because he rejects a semantic test of properties, the ethical naturalist denies that this necessary relation represents either logical or conceptual necessity; instead, it represents metaphysical necessity or necessity a posteriori.[10]

And according to Nicholas Sturgeon:

> Since we find it plausible to attribute causal efficacy and explanatory relevance to moral facts, why should we not conclude . . . that their supervenience on nonmoral facts is . . . like the supervenience of biological facts on physical and chemical ones, or

> (on a physicalist view) of psychological facts on neurological ones—a kind of "causal constitution" of the supervening facts out of the more basic ones, which allow them a causal efficacy inherited from that of the facts out of which they are constituted?[11]

Practical realism is not intended to be a theory of supervenience *if* by supervenience it is meant that facts have moral significance independently of practical reason. Compare the biological case. Biological properties, for example, might be said to supervene on physical and chemical phenomena whether or not there are intellects. They do not have biological significance only for thinkers. On the other hand, in the comprehension of the world that is morally relevant, the moral significance of the world has crucially to do with its comprehension by practical reason. This is the employment of reason that considers things in terms of conceptions of worth and what it is good to do, and that structures and orients deliberation and action in accord with this understanding. Moral values are supervenient in the sense that while not made by the mind or projected by it; nothing would have moral value in a world which did not include practical reasoners. There might be pain or delight or comfort or fear, but that is not the same as there being ethical value.

One of the appeals of supervenience to a realist is that if moral facts or properties are supervenient then recognition of them does not require inference. We can perceive them directly, as long as we know how to look. If moral features are constituted by nonmoral features or are "fixed" by them, we do not need to acquire nonmoral information and then make an inference from it to the moral features of a situation.[12] Practical realism is in agreement with supervenience approaches on that score; moral features can be recognized directly. That the recognition of moral features of situations is noninferential does not, of course, mean that there needn't be any inference about what to do. One can reason from the conception of moral features, as when it is plain that courage is called for, but deliberation is needed to determine what meets the ethical requirements of the situation. Or one noninferentially might recognize that complete honesty is the right course but also judge that care and sensitivity in how the truth is reported are necessary, and that can take some planning.

The merit of supervenience is that it locates ethical value in the world, something we cognitively respond to. Yet we do not want to take the action-guiding significance of moral features as a brute fact.

There needs to be connection to the practical employment of reason in order to get prescriptivity back into the picture. And so, if we are going to stick to the strategy of supervenience to identify how values are in the world, we need to acknowledge that they are supervenient on nonmoral features of the world but supervenient for practical reason. Otherwise, they would just be there, anyway, independent of how they counted for any practical being. In saying that values are supervenient for practical reasoners, we are not making them subjective. It is, instead, an acknowledgment that the presence of moral value in the world depends upon the presence of practical reasoners, but given their nature, the presence of ethical value is an objective matter cognitively ascertained.

Blackburn has written extensively on value supervenience as part of his project of quasi-realism, which involves projectivist supervenience. That view is an attempt to preserve the realistic-looking features of moral judging, discourse, and argument while avoiding what are claimed to be fatal problems with realist supervenience. The latter, he argues, won't do because, if supervenience is not a relation of entailment, the realist cannot explain why, if the occurrence of a set of naturalistic properties in one case determines a moral feature, the occurrence of them in another must also do so. Along the same lines, supervenience without entailment cannot explain why moral features *stay* as they are on the basis of the continued existence of the naturalistic state of affairs. His alternative is to explain the supervenience on the basis of attitudes: "Now it is not possible to hold an attitude to a thing because of its possessing certain properties and, at the same time, not hold that attitude to another thing that is believed to have the same properties."[13] Actually, I suspect people sometimes do that. If it is objected that, if they do that they are making a moral mistake by doing so, that is all right, but it is not evidence for projectivism; it is a point about moral consistency. Blackburn says that his approach has a "distinct advantage in being alone consistent with supervenience and lack of entailment."[14] Thus, "to think a moral proposition is true is to concur in an attitude to its subject."[15] There is moral truth; it is just not realist truth. This does not work because it just relocates the difficulty that Blackburn insisted afflicted realist supervenience.

In "How to be an Ethical Antirealist"[16] he argues that there is a naturalistic story to tell about the emergence of ethical commitments and stances, but this is not a story that involves reference to values.

The structure of ethical thought and discourse, with its assertion making, argument, refinement, reason giving, and so forth, has the form that the realist prizes and interprets as entailing beliefs about ethical facts. But it is a structure articulated on a basis that is noncognitive and naturalistic, in the sense that what initiates and sustains it are conative states, attitudes, and sensibility. We give its emergence a realist-looking shape and need not regard it as an error to do so. That is just what moral practice is and all that values could be. This is naturalism, but it is not a naturalist ontological account of moral facts as identical with or constituted by nonmoral facts. It is projectivist naturalism. That is, we can be naturalists about how ethics has come to have a place in our lives without also being naturalists or realists about what ethical values are. They are not part of the natural world.

The spirit of Blackburn's position is Humean, as he avows. In order to make sense of ethics, we do not have to *start* by grounding it in realism or antirealism. There is no substantive, explanatory role for transcendental commitments. We need, rather, to look at *ethics*, at ethical reasoning, choice, and argument and see what is needed to account for its sense and its role in our lives. If a naturalistic projectivism succeeds in this, it is not necessary to absorb it somehow into one or another global theory, realist or antirealist. As Blackburn says:

> According to me, there is only one proper way to take the question "On what does the wrongness of wanton cruelty depend?": as a moral question, with an answer in which no mention of our actual responses properly figures. There *would* be an external reading if realism were true. For in that case there would be a fact, a state of affairs (the wrongness of cruelty) whose rise and fall and dependency on others could be charted. But antirealism acknowledges no such state of affairs, and no such issue of dependency.[17]

For practical realism it is not a matter of cognition finding the fact and then finding the additional relation of dependence. Rather, it is a matter of achieving the right comprehension of how the facts figure in rational consideration of what is good to do or how it is good for circumstances to be.

Blackburn's general strategy in developing an expressivist antirealism "is to explain the practice of moralizing, using causal language, and so on, in terms only of our exposure to a thinner reality—a world which contains only some lesser states of affairs, to which we respond and in which we have to conduct our lives."[18] Projection is not a mistake, and the recognition that we are projecting is not a reason to "give up some or all of our tendency to practice as if evaluative commitments had truth conditions."[19] Finding out that we are projecting (in moral talk and causal talk, for example) does not undermine the assertoric features of discourse, requiring us to reinterpret it as "flirting with a false realism."[20] Projection is not false realism, to be diagnosed by an error theory. Blackburn says that the enterprise of showing this, "that even on anti-realist grounds there is nothing improper, nothing 'diseased' in projected predicates,"[21] is what he calls "the enterprise of *quasi-realism*." "The point is that it tries to earn, on the slender basis, the features of moral language (or of other commitments to which a projective theory might apply) which tempt people to realism."[22]

Blackburn explicitly denies that projectivism is in the end reductionist, that our statements about things are really statements about our minds, and that the truth of our claims are "mind-dependent." What we can do without, though, is commitment to faculties that detect moral properties (or modal properties or causes that reality allegedly exhibits). Standards of moral talk, modal talk, or causal talk can be truth-conditional and have the dignity of objectivity while being explained without the extravagances of realism. Besides, what would those extravagances afford us? According to Blackburn, if moral properties supervene on nonmoral properties, we succeed not in realistically accounting for moral properties but only in rendering them mysterious. The reason is that "it does not seem a matter of conceptual or logical necessity that any given total natural state of a thing gives it some particular moral quality. For to tell which moral quality results from a given natural state means using standards whose correctness cannot be shown by conceptual means alone. It means moralizing, and bad people moralize badly, but need not be confused."[23]

Conceptual analysis will not lead us directly from knowledge of natural properties to knowledge of moral properties. Moreover, if a truth of supervenience is necessary, then it obtains in all possible worlds. If it is not necessary, then it obtains in some worlds but not others. But there cannot be mixed worlds, worlds in which a property sometimes supervenes on a given base and sometimes does not. But if supervenience is not a logical or conceptual matter, it is a mystery why there should be a ban on mixed worlds, something the supervenience theorist would surely insist upon.

Blackburn eliminates the mystery by interpreting supervenience projectively rather than realistically. Taking A to be supervening, "when we announce the A-commitments we are projecting, we are neither reacting to a given distribution of A-properties, nor speculating about one. So the supervenience can be explained in terms of the constraints upon proper projection."[24]

Either realist supervenience is a logical relation, a relation of entailment (which it is not); or it is a nomological relation. But in the latter case it would be conceivable that the nonmoral, subvening properties should be present, but not the moral, supervening properties. But the point of a supervenience theory is to disallow this possibility.

The appeal of a supervenience version of naturalism is that it purports to supply an account of the objects moral judgments refer to and describe. Part of Mackie's critique of supervenient naturalisms is that they do not adequately explain how a moral feature is present because natural features are, how it could be of "anything that is supposed to have some objective moral quality . . . that [moral feature] is linked with its natural features."[25] This is both an ontological and an epistemological issue, since it is problematic how we could "see" the "consequential link" between them. Moreover, he argues, "on a naturalist analysis, moral judgements can be practical, but their practicality is wholly relative to desires or possible satisfactions of the person or persons whose actions are to be guided; but moral judgements seem to say more than this. This view leaves out the categorical quality of moral requirements."[26]

So there is a problem with respect to moral motivation as well. Blackburn's quasi-realism is one approach that might seem to address all of these problems together. We have moral concepts that are grounded in our sensibility and interests, and we regard the world on the basis of these concepts; and their being rooted in our sensibility and interests accounts for the motivational energy of moral judgments. In effect, we take moral qualities to be supervening, but they are projected. The "queerness" of their ontological status and prescriptivity is normalized, and so the epistemological problem is made tractable.

In response, one could argue, as Brink has, that supervenience involves synthetic necessity, of the sort explored by Kripke, Putnam, and others. The relation between the nonmoral and the moral is thus necessary but not semantic or conceptual.[27] Brink appeals to the work of Kripke and Putnam on treating necessity as a metaphysical notion and a matter that is not, in the case of supervenience, to be treated as a one of meaning; synonymy is not the test of property identity, "and meaning implication is neither a necessary nor a sufficient condition for either constitution or strong supervenience."[28]

But even these background metaphysical and semantic considerations won't secure a successful account of moral supervenience. Realism won't give us supervening moral qualities without the teleology of practical reason. Those nonmoral facts and properties would not constitute moral considerations in the absence of practical reason. With respect to ethics, explanatorily they would, in that case, count for nothing. The supervenience of ethical values involves practical reasoners not in the sense that the values "come from" us but in the sense that there are ethical values only for practical reasoners.

One reason projectivist supervenience is unsatisfactory is that it does not provide a satisfactory account of what makes sound ethical judgment sound. It won't do to pick out in some very general way human propensities and attitudes and say that our theorizing is supported by their substance and is a realist-looking working out of them. The ones selected will be either too general, not supporting one set of judgments rather than another, or too specific, relying on what is already elaborated moral theory. It remains unclear why certain judgments are sound and others not, in the absence of cognitivist determination of them. And it won't do simply to say that this matter needs no further explanation, that we are already there in the midst of a naturalistically sustained moral world.

While the antirealist can point to the mysteries of realist supervenience and prescriptivity, projectivist antirealism leaves it a mystery why certain responses should constitute or ground authoritative commitments, why they should be taken as normative rather than (more thinly) just plain dispositional. The projectivist could point to the phenomenology of certain responses and say, "But to see how they figure in our judgments and our actions and our lives is to see that they are constitutive of morality." But this is not something that can be read off the projected responses any more than it can be read off or synthetically identified with nonmoral facts.

For example, it would be wrong to push the baby out of the high chair. What sort of understanding is this? It is true that it would be bad for the baby to fall out of the high chair, and its being true depends upon facts about babies and falls. The dependence is not analytic. Neither is the badness a function of a Humean custom of mind or passion. It is something objective for practical reason. This objectivity is internal to practical reason in the sense that the badness of a fall is not detected by theoretical reason and then turned over to practical reason in order to do something with it. But something is lost if we follow the Blackburn-Hume approach and jettison realist concerns about whether our judgments answer to the world. "Answering to" can, for practical reason, be a registering and acknowledgment of a kind of significance that is at the same time factual and reason-giving. And this sort of registering and acknowledgment is what is discussed and argued about in ethical talk, or at least ethical talk that has as its aim the articulation of why certain responses to, decisions about, and identifications of what ethically matters are rationally endorsable.

As was argued earlier, we only act at all because we have desires, we are beings with appetites, inclinations, and felt needs. But it would be a mistake to conclude from this that reason is a handmaiden in action, that both end and motive are fully or primarily determined by desire. That desire has an essential role in action neither derationalizes the end or motive nor dissolves the realism of ethical value. The notion of sound dispositions or correct propensities is crucial to morality and is explicated in terms of rational considerations, and realist ones at that. Desire is not cognition, but if we separate desire too sharply from reason, we are left to wonder how it is that we form tendencies to judge and appreciate situations as providing reasons for action. We understand situations as supplying this or that reason for action because we are practical beings, beings who think in terms of what is to be done and what the worth of it is. That we think *this way* at all is because desire is essential to us, and that we *think* this way is because desire can be shaped and directed by reason. Projection is not what makes for value. Things matter to us because of what we are like; or rather, given our nature, things have objective ethical significance. Projectivism, in a way, gets things the wrong way round. We do not find what we put out there and then claim that it was really there (or that it is as if it was really there) on its own. Rather, what's there (not necessarily in the sense of "external" but in the sense of what is realistically the case) ethically matters in certain rationally specifiable ways because of what we are like.

It might be supposed that to validate the realism of this view, then, surely some facts must be morally relevant in themselves and thus moral facts *do* constitute a distinct category. If they do not, how are we to ascertain where ethical significance lies? But this is a mistake. There isn't a special property that makes some facts morally significant. We cannot state in a completely general, systematic way which facts are morally significant and in just what way. The moral significance of the fact that someone is blind depends upon what kinds of situations they are in. The fact that a medical procedure is very painful has no fixed moral significance; its significance depends upon whether there are equally effective alternative treatments, whether anesthetics are available, and so forth. We cannot set out in advance what moral significance facts will have, though of course there is a great deal of accumulated practical wisdom and well-supported generalizations. Realism is committed to the facts being ethically significant, not to there being a unique set of ethically significant facts.

Moreover, moral claims need not be fitted into a system in order to express practical knowledge. A judgment can be right, and nonaccidentally right, even if the judger cannot justify it by appeal to higher-level principles. Being a good judge of ethical matters does not require an ability to specify criteria of good judgment and also to show that they are satisfied.

Chisholm distinguishes between "methodists" and "particularists" in epistemology, the former insisting on an answer to the question "What are the criteria of knowledge?" as a prerequisite to answering the question "What do we know?" and the latter working out the answers the other way round.[29] A great deal of modern moral theory is methodist. An ethic in which practical wisdom is central is much more likely to be particularist. Practical cognition typically takes as its object features of quite particular situations, and a practical cognition can be valid without being derived. This does not mean that nothing can be said about what makes it correct. An account of the correctness of the claim will connect it up with many other considerations. But someone's recognition of the wrongness of kidnapping and killing a child does not need derivation from first principles in order to be a genuine, knowing recognition. If the person has well-ordered sensibility and is able to employ the relevant concepts, they can get this judgment right and nonaccidentally be right in doing so.

The example above is an action-type that it is safe to say is always wrong, and this may seem to conflict with what was said in the prior paragraph. But it is more an exception that proves the rule. Recall Aristotle, who says that

> not every action nor every passion admits of a mean; for some have names that already imply badness, e.g., spite, shamelessness, envy, and in the case of actions adultery, theft, murder; for all of these and such like things imply by their names that they are themselves bad, and not the excesses or deficiencies of them. It is not possible, then, ever to be right with regard to them; one must always be wrong. (*N.E.* 1107a 9–14)

Even if we do not endorse the doctrine of the mean, and even if we dispute Aristotle's examples, we can accept the point of this: some action-types are always wrong. But, for one thing, the list is relatively short, compared to the number of action-types there are, and for another, that some are always wrong is not a conclusion arrived at by a theoretical derivation. A person could know that theft is wrong without this being the conclusion of a justifying argument. Indeed, Aristotle gives none. An agent with good character knows this, and acts on this knowledge. The story about why theft is wrong can be told, and it refers to facts about human needs and purposes. And if it is not *always* wrong, there is a factual explanation about that, too. But high-level moral principles do not precede, and are not prerequisites for, practical knowledge.

PRACTICAL REALISM AND INTERNAL REALISM

Skepticism about reason's ability to achieve conceptions of good, typically goes together with skepticism about its motivational efficacy. Thus we are left with an account of both value and motivation rooted in an agent's dispositions or their subjective motivational set.[30] It is not as if, for things to *really* matter, they must matter independently of us. Indeed, it is very obscure what that could even *mean*. Things really do matter; the hard part is producing an account of how they *rightly* matter. They really matter for us, given that we are practical reasoners capable of action guided by understanding. That is as real as mattering or values can be.

Mackie's claim that objective values, in their having to be prescriptive, would be queer, turns on taking values to be entities or properties and then stopping to wonder how their imperative force could possibly operate. This is analogous to wondering how something could matter but not matter *to* anyone. Could there be mattering if there were no aims, interests, or desires? Suppose there were intellects, but without these things. What sort of cognition would they need in order to have knowledge that this or that mattered? Put in this way, both the metaphysics and the epistemology of values do seem deeply problematic and ripe for skepticism. And formulating the issue in this way raises issues similar to those raised by Putnam in his critique of metaphysical realism; i.e., we seem to be attributing to things in the world not only mindlike attributes but attributes of practical mind, including motivational power and a built-in logic of right action.

Given this account of practical realism, it may sound something like an ethical version of Putnam's internal realism, a realism with a small *r*, in which the mind has an essential role in constituting objects. But this is not internal realism, for all of the centrality of the activity of practical reason in it. We do make concepts by which we comprehend objects, and the concepts enable us to recognize the ethical significance of facts. But this is not significance that the mind attributes to facts by projection, nor does the mind construct moral facts. While antirealists such as Blackburn undertake to explain what needs to be explained about ethics without any realist commitments, Putnam's internal realism is motivated by what he takes to be incoherencies in externalism. It would, he claims, involve there being self-identifying objects, reference to them unmediated by conceptual choices, and a relation of correspondence to determine truth-values that he regards as impossible because it cannot be shown to be determinate.[31]

Moreover, Putnam argued that notions of explanatory salience, modality, and causality are mind-dependent. It is, he holds, incoherent to attribute them to things in themselves, since this would involve attributing mindlike characteristics to things. Natural kinds, causal relations, modal properties, and so forth, are not "out there" in some self-identifying manner that the mind can represent in cognition of them. For example, "if events *intrinsically* explain other events, if there are saliencies, relevancies, standards of what are 'normal' conditions, and so on, built into the world itself independently of minds then the world is in many ways *like* a mind, or infused with something very much like reason."[32]

Realism does not require that the world be infused with mindlike characteristics. It requires that the world be intelligible, that our conceptualizations be cognitive actualizations of an order of things independent of them. Moral realism and realism in general do not require that a thought be a re-presentation of what is so, each representation being a copy of a fact. Our cognition does not simply copy facts of prescriptivity or facts of causal relevance. It is probably helpful to drop the idiom of "representation" for these kinds of matters, since it so easily motivates questions concerning copying and resembling. Rather, we should interpret cognition in terms of conceptual actualization or realization. Comprehension is not a matter of there being a distinct impression or copy of its referent. We can, in a world guided manner, achieve understandings and recognitions of things through our conceptualizations being true to what is intelligible. Cognition just is the capacity for this.[33] We can comprehend the causal or prescriptive significance of some situation without there being distinct facts of "being the cause of" or "being ethically required" that are mentally copied. What is causally explanatory and what is ethically required can be comprehended without the comprehension being a one-to-one relation between a representation and a fact.

It is not altogether clear just how Putnam's internal realism essentially differs from some forms of idealism. It is like them in that it holds that the notion of a world order existing independently of conceptualization and schemes of description is an idle or incoherent notion. It also rejects correspondence truth. Though Putnam insists that there are "experiential *inputs* to knowledge,"[34] he denies that "there are any inputs *which are not themselves to some extent shaped by our concepts*, . . ."[35] Unless one accepts Putnam's model-theoretic argument against realist theories of reference as both non-question-begging and relevant, it is not clear how effective the claim in the quotation is. The fact that something must be conceptualized in order for it to figure in our understanding or knowledge of the world does not imply that what it is depends upon that conceptualization. The larger point though, is that it is a mistake to interpret the world as a plastic medium having organization and containing definite kinds only on a scheme of conceptualization and within a system of intentions to refer. Our classifications and descriptions are responses to what we find and the rightness of our conceptions depends upon the order of things independent of them. Putnam's claim is that there is no question of comparing or mapping concepts to a mind-independent reality. We can agree with that. The contention is not that there is comparison but that what mind comprehends are the objects and features it encounters. Cognition is not a matter of matching thought to object; it is a conceptual actualization of what is intelligible.

In any case, practical realism is not a strategy of domesticating ethical value to mind if that means ethical value is a construction or projection. There are not self-identifying ethical facts of the matter, but there is realist comprehension of ethical significance. The content and truth of ethical claims depend upon what are the realistically interpreted facts. The facts matter to ethical description and to ethical reasons analogously to the way realist facts matter to causal explanations; by being their reference and the grounds of their truth-value.

One specific reason that practical realism may seem like an ethical version of internal realism is that facts count as ethical considerations only because we are practical beings. So the general nature of human desire and sensibility has a place in the explication of ethical considerations. In that respect, our nature is essential to what we ethically find in the world. This is still realism, though, because the facts and situations that are the grounds of ethical considerations are to be interpreted realistically, the goods that practical reasoning understands are realistic goods for us, and ethical claims have realist truth-values. What would be mysterious is if reason were a capacity to intuit modal, causal, and ethical properties of objects that we could refer to in a reliably determinate way without conceptualizing and theorizing. But realism is not committed to that. The ethical significance of facts, like the explanatoriness of them in nonethical contexts, is formulated by reason and expressed in language. But it is a realistically referential language, and ethical and explanatory significance depends upon truth-conditions that are not wholly determined by our conceptual choices and linguistic practices.

Putnam's critique of realism is mainly a critique of what he takes to be metaphysical realism, the thesis that there is a mind-independent world of objects that we can refer to and to which true propositions correspond. Realism has been understood in different ways; Dummett has characterized it in more directly semantic terms. He says that in statements about a disputed class of things,

> for the realist, we have assigned a meaning to these statements in such a way that we know, for each such statement, what has to be the case for it to be true. . . . The condition for the truth of a statement is not, in general, a condition which we are capable of recognizing as obtaining whenever it obtains, or even one for which we have an effective procedure for determining whether it obtains or not.[36]

Dummett's characterization flows from considerations about meaning that lead him to endorse a version of verificationism. Putnam's characterization has different starting points, and he is anxious to avoid being identified as a verificationist. He describes truth in terms of ideal justification; and it is correspondence that centrally concerns him, rather than the evidence-transcendence or recognition-transcendence of realist truth-conditions. But there is still an important commonality in their views. Both deny the claim that statements are made true by facts of the matter independent of our concepts, beliefs, and evidence.

While antirealists often take the very formulation of realism to exhibit directly its untenability (especially concerning correspondence), antirealism itself is faced with serious difficulties of its own making. For example, do not the minds that do the representing have some nature "in themselves"? As Wolterstorff has claimed of some forms of antirealism:

> If the world as such has no constitution of things and kinds and facts, if whatever has a constitution has been constituted by us, then the self and its version-constituting activity are also part of the version it constitutes. Accordingly, it does not belong to the constitution of the world that there are human beings who constitute world versions. . . . The fact that the world has no constitution apart from us is not a fact about the world apart from us. It too is nothing more than a feature of our way of constituting the world.[37]

And Bonjour, commenting on the antirealist rejection of metaphysical realism, says: "But only a moment's reflection will show that such a view is incoherent if adopted as a general thesis about reality: not everything can have reality only as the object of an act of thought or representation, for the representative act must itself exist *an sich* if it is to confer representative reality on its object."[38]

If realism is open to the objection that accounting for just what *really* are the kinds or facts that are in the world appears beyond its reach, antirealism is certainly open to the even more disturbing worry that it appears to try to have things both ways, claiming that what things there are depend upon us in a fundamental way but that there is not anything "in itself" that we are that could explain the possibility of this. On the more clearly semantic issue, it is doubtful that antirealism can succeed in sustaining notions of reference and assertion that are adequate to explain or support the activity of statement making without involving realism somewhere in the account. Even if we shift from truth-conditions to verification-conditions, the latter will need to be interpreted realistically. Or if we go in for assertibility under optimal conditions (the Putnam move) it is still difficult to see what this sort of justification could count for unless it were justification because it brings us closer to the truth.[39] If justification is not realistically truth-conducive, it is unclear what its significance is either epistemically or metaphysically. The move to interpreting truth as assertibility under ideal conditions (are *they* realistically construed?) co-opts it in a way that mortgages its authority. That skepticism is a possibility on realist grounds is not a decisive objection to realism. It is an acknowledgment that we cannot eliminate possibilities by distracting ourselves with other things. The independence of truth from justification does not put truth out of reach; it enables it to retain its authority for credentialing methods of justification. One has to be a realist about something. It won't do to explain truth in terms of justification, since that would rob truth of independent significance and, as a consequence, rob justification of truth-related significance.

Even if we are confident in realism, practical realism may appear to have peculiarities of its own that are problematic. If there are unrecognized ethical truths, then wouldn't there be, so to speak, undischarged prescriptivity? How could that be? It has already been argued that prescriptivity is not an intrinsic feature of facts independent of their comprehension by practical reason. It is not that there is "ought-to-be-doneness" (Mackie's expression) out there in the world. Whether we think of such a thing as at work or idling, it is pretty mysterious. Prescriptivity is not an object, any more than "explains" is a term that refers to an object. Realism about ethical considerations concerns the manner in which considerations count as reasons; it does not require commitment to exotic objects. Prescriptivity is not a subjective matter except in that it does not exist apart from practical reasoners. When we explain to someone his error in judgment we are bringing to light prescriptive significance that he missed. And when at the more general, social level moral concepts are articulated and revised, the same sort of thing is happening. If there are facts and practical reasoners, then those facts are considerations with prescriptive significance for those reasoners. We can stand by this without having to interpret facts antirealistically or as internally realist. The facts are not constituted by practical reason, and the recognition of ethical relevance and import has as its referential base a world order that includes us but is not dependent upon us. We should not confuse, on the one hand, ethical significance being "made up" by practical reason and, on the other, it being understood by it. Understanding reason-giving significance is not representation of built-into-the-world prescriptivity. It could not be that. Prescriptivity (as opposed to other kinds of motive force) entails taking something to be a reason. This is not to say that nothing could count as a reason unless it was in fact taken to be such, but that it is on account of reason (reason's being practical) that something can figure in an ethical judgment or decision about what to do. Prescriptivity concerns rational authority, not just motive power (or a willingness to universalize). Why should prescribing even count as registering a norm for a rational agent if it is not at least potentially rationally authoritative, assessable in terms of soundness as a course or policy of action with respect to how the world is?

Suppose a pile of logs falls off the back of a truck and some of them land on someone. It is a fact that the logs have fallen, it is a fact that some of them are on top of someone, and it is a fact that that person is in distress. It is also a fact that it would be good to help him. This is not another fact "on the pile," so to speak. But the features of the situation as understood by practical reason are the considerations that explain its being a good thing that the person should be helped. Is it good in itself that the person be helped? The phrase "in itself" here needn't have any mysterious metaphysical sense. It is objectively good that the person be helped, and this is understood by practical reason. For that matter, *helping* is something understood by practical reason; it is a concept of practical reason. Helping is something an agent does. It is a causal notion, but one embedded in rational action. We do correctly say things such as "A bit more rain would help the crops," but this is a notion tied to our practical concerns and concepts, even though, in a sense detached from them, it refers to a natural causal process. In the primary sense of "helping," it is a notion that gets its criteria from considerations interpreted by practical reason.

The ethical significance of facts is not always unambiguous, or only of one type, or evident even to attentive, careful, ethically sophisticated people. But it is the facts that are morally significant; they are the objects of moral awareness and thought. Ethical thought is a crucial element in our being at home in the world through understanding it. This is not a matter of some providential or magical ordering of our nature with a good subsisting independently of it. It is reason's engagement with the world and our own nature in its capacity to comprehend and realize what is good. Figuring out what to do is a project for practical reason.

The well-ordering of practical reason comes about through action, habit, deliberation, and experience. As form can only be realized in matter receptive to it, so, too, can sound practical comprehension be achieved only by a person who is to some extent apt to achieve it through natural and acquired dispositions. Still, a substantial element of it is a certain kind of generalized attention to the world: an aspiration to recognize and appreciate the normative significance of facts, a practical counterpart to the kind of attention of theoretical reason that seeks explanation and intelligibility. In large part, this is a willingness to look outward, to find for practical reason objects and motives other than the desires or feelings one happens to have, and so to revise and reorient one's desires and feelings with a concern for a more objective, nuanced, and responsive conception of what it is good to do and why.

Wiggins' SENSIBLE SUBJECTIVISM

An account of well-ordered practical reason is so important because it is an account of the right appreciation of the normative significance of factual considerations. We do not (properly) "make up" values or project them onto the facts. Values depend upon the normative significance of our circumstances and our constitution—our abilities, propensities, and susceptibilities. What is a human good or a generalized human interest is a matter of what human beings *are*, not a matter of what their desires and responses *happen* to be. What practical reason rightly understands is not just "true for us" in a subjectivist sense if that means that it is not world-guided, given the world and our nature. It is realistically true, given what we are.

This view might sound close to Wiggins' view in "A Sensible Subjectivism?" There he argues that sensibility and properties can be brought into a kind of coordination or harmony where they are recognized as made for each other. He argues that in a sensible subjectivism "there is still a place for the sentient subject . . . this is a subjectivism of subjects and properties *mutually* adjusted."[40] But

> we are surely not committed to suppose that the properties that figure within these <property, response> pairs will bear to natural properties any relation of supervenience that could be characterized in terms that were both general and illuminating of the particular properties in question. Rather they will be primi-

> tive, sui generis, incurably anthropocentric, and as unmysterious as any properties will ever be to us.[41]

This is not Humean subjectivism, nor is it a brand of naturalism or realism. In his view, our actual responses do not constitute moral properties; nor do those properties have an ontological status independent of our sensitivity to certain properties. Wiggins' position is an attempt, largely Wittgensteinian in character, to overcome subject-object and word-world dualisms. For example, he says that "the sort of agreement that is in question here is only agreement in *susceptibility* to respond thus and so to ϕ things. It is agreement at most (as one might say, evoking a very familiar passage of Wittgenstein) in what property/response associations we are able to catch onto and work up into a shared way of talking, acting and reacting."[42]

For this kind of subjectivism, moral judgments are not expressions of feelings, they are genuine judgments; criteria of correctness apply to them, and they can be criticized and rationally revised. Moral values are not items set out for us there in the world, and they are not reducible to actual responses people happen to have. In making moral judgments and applying moral predicates, we are not referring to something outside of us, something not "*conscious subject*-involving."[43] But neither are we driving out objects and properties from what we are talking about and confining the content of moral judgment to what is registered by sentiment considered on its own, just as felt. Moral rationality is not based on Moorean cognition or eliminated by emotivist or prescriptivist analysis. The strategy seems to be that if we can give up insisting on a clean break between subject and object, we can find that features of both are implicated in moral thinking and the constitution of values. This is an antireductive strategy. That is a merit of Wiggins' view. And practical realism shares with it the claim that an appraiser of the appropriate sort will morally approve of certain properties. The response and the property are indeed intimately related. But the difficulty is over how to explicate the notion of "an appraiser of the *appropriate* sort." The notion of "mutual adjustment" of property and response needs to do a great deal of explanatory work, and it is not clear how it is done. The appeal to Wittgenstein lends some illumination by association, but not enough to bring the real workings of the account to light. Blackburn, for example, says of Wiggins' position that it is a "Whiggish one" and one that "is often in place," but that it is itself a moral judgment and not pertinent to explaining *how* sensibilities are "made for values."[44] It is in place; the unclarity is in how it got there. Blackburn, as we have seen, would appeal to a projectivist explanation, but we have rejected that. Cognitivist simulacra are not enough to justify moral judgments. The respect in which values are "*conscious subject*-involving" is not exclusively or primarily in terms of sensibility but, rather, in terms of cognitively credentialed notions of appropriate response. Wiggins calls his view a "cognitivist formulation of subjectivism" and insists that in it response is neither a "criterion" nor even an "indicator" but is part of judgment that is "sustained by the perceptions and feelings and thoughts that are open to criticism that is based on norms that are open to criticism."[45] This too is congenial to practical realism, but in it "mutual adjustment" is replaced or explicated in terms of recognition of truth. What is practical truth is in part a matter of the nature of the agent; and so this is subject-involving. It is facts about the nature of the agent or subject that explain the naturalness or appropriateness of moral judgments. Some of these facts concern sensibility, but they are among the objects of cognitive assessment. And in *making* moral judgments, sensibility is involved, but involved in a way that can be cognitively informed and directed. It is not just that a judgment can "rest upon sentiment *and* relate to a matter of fact."[46] Rather, judgment can rest on sentiment motivated or disposed by an understanding of the facts.

It is not clear how the cognitivism of the view Wiggins describes escapes, on the one hand, being absorbed into Wittgensteinian realism-through-language-and-practice or, on the other, being a kind of supervenient cognitivism. By this I mean that features of cognitivism are superadded onto a projectivist or subjectivist base. Wiggins does say that he does not wish to identify his position as "*realism,* as if to contrast it with *mentalism* or whatever."[47] There are *whatevers,* such as quasi-realism, which it seems to be close to, and because of this his position's claim to cognitivism needs very cautious consideration. But the issue is not labeling, it is the adequacy of the position. And I have indicated reasons for questioning it on that score.

Practical reason itself needs to be well ordered in certain ways in order to achieve sound comprehensions of ethical significance, and here is where susceptibilities or dispositions do figure crucially in the development of the ability to make and understand correct judgments. Again the view borrows from Aristotle in its acknowledgment of the crucial importance of emotion and desire being disposed in ways that agree with what reason asserts, even prior to one's own understanding being mature and self-conscious. These dispositions, as Aristotle claimed, are almost certainly largely a matter of habituation. But it need not be exclusively a matter of that; and adult experience, insights, and "conversions" of various sorts, coming to see things in new ways, can also affect the agreement of sensibility, desire, and reason. A good deal of the "fit" that is achieved is not so much a matter of fitting subject to object but of understanding, on the one hand, and sensibility and desire, on the other, being brought into agreement. Practical reason's object is the realization or achievement of what is good in action, and the cultivation of the passions is crucial to the individual's perceptions and ability to understand. But the passions are not the basis of what it is good to do, nor are they the sole source of prescriptivity. Reason will not do its practical work well in the absence of susceptibilities and propensities being oriented by habit to attend to its objects. We will say more about this in the next chapter and in the conclusion. Both what it is good to do and the motive to do it depend upon reason as a capacity to understand and as a capacity to order the passions. Rational dispositions to act entail responding to something (the facts) but are not merely passional responses.

DISCLOSURE AND SIGNIFICANCE

To what extent does realism help us understand moral argument or explanation? If someone does not recognize that cruelty and slander are wrong, what do they need to know? It is not a matter of presenting them with a special piece of information, a moral fact. The person needs to come to see an act *as* an act that is wrong; but this is not seeing something else, but seeing-as. People who do see cruelty or slander as wrong possess concepts and recognitional abilities that a person "blind" to the situation, or seeing it differently, lacks. Their seeing-as is an exercise of judgment, a cognitive act, and not a reflection, expression, or projection of something noncognitive. This is like the case where someone sees a curveball being thrown, not just a pitch or a thrown object. There aren't more facts for that person, but he recognizes more fully what the facts are. If someone denies that the throw was a pitch in a baseball game or denies that it was a curveball, he has made a mistake. Similarly with perceptions of the wrongness of cruelty. Neither our feelings about cruelty nor our saying it is wrong make it wrong. Failure to judge cruelty wrong is not a failure of projection. It can be interpreted as a moral failure, but it is a failure of moral cognition.

The ethical concepts that we employ when we make ethical judgments do not simply appear to be cognitive because of our being accustomed to their use, because we use them to describe and make assertions. Consider how the use of ethical concepts is learned. We are taught to make judgments by focusing our attention on certain features of acts, situations, and characteristics, and we are taught to notice analogies and similarities and to identify and articulate the considerations that support ethical judgments. Learning may often take the form of internalizing rules, but applying them is a matter of attending to and judging particular situations. Mature ethical judgment is less rule-oriented and more a matter of appreciating what the facts of situations count for. The more subtle and fine-grained our attention, the more is disclosed to us and the more we can disclose to others by way of description and instruction.[48] Our affective responses can be more and more in agreement with cognition by being informed by what we perceive. The education of sensibility can follow conceptual and judgmental articulation.

We can come to have habits of response (both affective and cognitive) by having ethical significance disclosed by others. The disclosure is a matter of achieving an understanding, and the understanding can revise our attitudes and feelings. What is disclosed is a way of taking facts as reasons for ethical judgment and action, and in having this disclosed we are better able to explain the correctness of judgments. Disclosure figures in knowledge generally. For example, coming to recognize the flight of birds as migratory behavior, indicating the onset of a change in season, is an appreciation of significance attained by disclosure. What is disclosed is the intelligibility of what is experienced. Disclosure is not a mysterious property of some sorts of "special" experience. It is a pervasive feature of learning, experience, and the acquisition of concepts. It is part of coming to perceive things for what they are, and it often has import that is quite extensive. For example, in coming to recognize the flight of birds as migratory behavior, one may well be led to ask about the behavior of other animals or the changes in plants as evidence of seasonal change or indications of environmental conditions. One disclosure of significance can lead to other changes in perception and additional and finer discriminations in perceiving-things-as. The intelligibility of several things in the world can be brought into view by it. Disclosure and perceiving-as function in the same general way in ethical experience. We can come to see certain kinds of acts as unfair or selfish, or certain characteristics as vices, and we can come to understand them as wrong or as bad. The heightening or articulation of sensibility that often attends this is neither an antecedently necessary condition for it nor constitutive of it. And besides, the explanation of the change in sensibility includes reference to the cognitively recognized features of what motivates the changes.[49]

A similar sort of thing occurs in a person's coming to appreciate art or music. Their sensibility is vitalized and organized by their increased understanding. We can learn how to see a painting or listen to a piece of music, "learn how" in the sense that we learn to discern structure, subtlety, and detail. As a result, our feelings are engaged in new ways. We find emotions in ourselves as a result of understanding, and we also can come to have new desires, desires to perceive, appreciate, and feel certain ways.

The notion of disclosure is applicable across a wide range of experience and learning, and in many of these contexts it plainly involves a cognitive element. We either acquire new concepts or learn to use concepts in new ways in making noninferential judgments. Think of how a concept like unfair resentment or forgiveness is learned. Learning such concepts is an experiential, practical matter. Sometimes just being told, "Look, you're being resentful, you haven't got good reasons for your bitterness, you just want to blame him for your frustration" can awaken us to a way of seeing a situation and a characteristic of ourselves. The awakening can lead to a change in our feelings and a reconsideration of how we see ourselves and other people.

Habituation often occurs, at least in part, through the experience of disclosure situations. A disclosure is almost never confined in its significance to the particular situation in which it occurs. When significance is disclosed, *we* are changed through learning to perceive something new. We might then reassess numerous other situations and experiences and also be enabled to make a new range of judgments. Our repertoire of recognitional abilities is broadened, deepened, or made more subtle, and as such it is better suited to the texture of the realities it is deployed upon.

The disclosure of significance can lead to the formation of a habit of mind, where this involves cognition, perception, and emotion or desire. If we come to recognize the wrongness of a certain kind of action, we can then come to be angered by it and to want to do something about it when we encounter it. Disclosures of significance by which one comes to an ethical appreciation of something are not "purely" cognitive in that they are not simply disclosures of the truth of propositions. They are disclosures that affect us *practically*, reconfiguring emotionality and desire. We come to care about something or care about it in a different way, and in a manner that involves practical dispositions. Actually, this is also often part of disclosure of theoretical matters as well. For example, once a person has the experience of understanding how to solve certain kinds of algebraic equations, she may develop an appetite for doing that kind of mathematics or mathematics generally. The enjoyment and the appetite accompany the understanding. This and the ethical examples are indicative of the truth in Aristotle's claim that the well-functioning, the good activity of a capacity is naturally pleasing. This idea will be taken up more fully later on.

We should briefly consider how to respond to the skeptic who challenges the claim that there has been a disclosure. The skeptic may challenge its validity, insisting that we are misperceiving something or claiming to perceive something that in fact is not really there at all. In some kinds of cases, if a person challenges a claim of significance of an experience, it is simply because he does not "get it" or "see it." His being unmoved passionally and being cognitively uncomprehending go hand in hand. If he asks, "How do you know those birds are migrating because of the change of season, and not just flying around together?" there is a factual story we can tell him, and unless he is just being irritatingly obtuse, he will "get it" even if doing so does not fire any interest in or appreciation of nature. In the aesthetic and ethical contexts, transmission of disclosure may be more difficult. But the persistence of a challenge is not necessarily evidence of the weakness of the claim being challenged. A morally disordered individual may just not "get it," may have dispositions so entrenched that they are, as it were, unregenerate. The person may not care to get it if, for example, he is so comfortable with his callousness—it is so completely second nature—that he just does not recognize the misfortune and suffering of others as a reason to aid or console them. It can be like arguing with a two year old. Or he may have a more self-conscious, reasoned way of disputing the claim of significance. He may have reasons for appreciating the situation differently, disputing whether, for example, it really is a case of unfairness. Here, as in most contexts, there is a real difference between good judgment and bad. The idea that, in order for a claim to be justified, the maker must be able to convince a skeptical challenger that it is justified is not very compelling. For one thing, people with good ethical judgment may not be able to articulate just what good judgment consists in. They may be right without knowing a justifying argument that shows that they are right. Someone can recognize styles of musical composition without knowing music theory, and someone can be a reliable judge of ethical matters without being able to present accounts of the rightness of her judgments. She will be able to say something, but that is not the same thing as having an argument effective at overcoming a skeptical challenge. And it is not necessary that she should.

Persons who do not correctly judge ethical matters because they lack the required conceptual abilities or because their desires and sensibility are not of the right sort may very well be unmoved by argument or explanation. Argument and explanation can be important to moral education and to bringing people to have the right practical conceptual and perceptual abilities and moral sensibility. But especially in practical matters it is a mistake to think the truth of ethical propositions alone will bring conviction about ethical matters. The transmission of values is almost never a matter of passing along propositions, even when the vehicle of transmission is an argument that supports them. Receptivity is also needed, and receptivity is in part made possible by habituation.

Many challenges to ethical claims lose their apparent force as challenges to the truth of those claims once it is recognized that the person issuing the challenge is the sort of person not apt to accept such a claim. This point can be abused, in obvious ways. But it is an important point that the ethical characteristics of the challenger and the challenged make a difference. A young person with good habits of attention and response can be right about many ethical matters but at a loss to present reasoning in defense of his actions and judgments. A more mature person can perhaps fit his judgment into a larger account and can give some reasons. But being ethically well ordered is a practical matter, a matter of having dispositions to judge, choose, and weigh things, and being that way is not the same thing as having a theory of what it is to be that way. The lack of a theory is not a ground for denying that the person is correct and responsible in his judgments.

So, who is involved in a situation of ethical argument or explanation makes a difference to what sorts of considerations will be telling. The state of the participants is not simply given at the outset: we are not confined to "preaching to the converted." Disclosure can occur in the process, and changes in view are possible, changes motivated by new understanding. But the force of ethical considerations can be deflected by bad character. The fact that ethical considerations do not convince someone is not, as such, an indication of the considerations being less than sound or justified.

ETHICAL DESCRIPTION

In saying that something is wrong or is fair, for example, are we describing it? Well, description is not just one thing. When we say, "That tree is an oak" or "That tree is deciduous," we are describing it, or at least these are perfectly in order as parts of an answer to the question "Can you describe that tree next to the stone wall?" These are descriptive sentences even though they are descriptions supported and credentialed by a system of concepts and classificatory categories, as are "There goes a mechanized battalion" and "The representative from Texas spoke out of turn." Ethical language or the use of language in ethically relevant ways is often descriptive in a fairly noncontroversial sense. If we hear of cruel and abusive treatment of someone and say, "That sort of thing is wrong, whatever they were disagreeing about," its being wrong can be explicated in terms of the facts of the case without decomposition into some nonassertoric meaning. Or when someone says, "I see now that what I did was vindictive and inappropriate," this, too, gets its meaning and correctness from the facts. This is so even though a notion like appropriateness may depend upon a potentially very complex and textured web of institutions, practices, and attitudes. Consider "courageous," "benevolent," "unselfish," "callous," "insincere," "invidious," "dishonest," "shameful." All of these have ethically relevant uses, and their uses are not tied to some one common meaning or criterion. What is common to them is that they are concepts that in their application also indicate reasons for certain kinds of action or response. Ethical uses of concepts involve judging the facts of the matter as considerations of practical reason. The use of ethical terms can safely be regarded as descriptive as long as we do not take this to presuppose some clean break between description and evaluation or between cognitive meaning and emotive meaning and as long as we recognize that there is a practical comprehension of things or an understanding of the world by practical reason.

In our practical consideration of the world, we don't first describe it and then join to the description some valuational accessory that renders it relevant to action. Practical thought is action-relevant in itself, regarding the world in terms of prescriptivity. The task of practical reasoning is to achieve right ethical description, not to join to ethically neutral description some independent conative or motivational state.

It makes sense to speak of ethical misdescriptions as a way of referring to incorrect assessments and judgments, and whether something is ethically misdescribed depends upon perception and comprehension of facts. In this respect ethical description is not essentially different from description that concerns causality or kind-membership. When we describe something as a cause of something else, we're not just reading this off the facts, nor are we projecting it onto them. We employ concepts that enable us to make certain kinds of identifications and discriminations even though "being a cause of" or "being a member of kind K" is not a sensory "given." In these kinds of cases, as in ethical cases, the correctness of the description depends upon how the world is. Where ethical description differs is in its relation to providing reasons for action.

If I am to deliberate well about what to do, if I am to choose an ethically sound act to perform, I need a right description of the circumstances that action and judgment are concerned with. Getting more facts is not just more information for me to respond to in a basically noncognitive way. It is material for a more accurate and informed practical cognition. When we say, "Oh, if I had known that, I would have acted differently," we may be indicating that our description of the situation would have been different as an ethical description. Different concepts would have applied, and given that, we would have recognized reasons for acting differently.

An individual's practical understanding can be enlarged by exercises in moral imagination as well as by encounters with novel situations. We can explore moral possibilities and amplify our concepts by various types of speculative consideration. In this way, we can test the suitability and limitations of our vocabulary and perceptions and perhaps come to see that, given our present or previous repertoire of abilities, certain kinds of ethical significance have gone unnoticed by us. In this sense, moral considerations can go unrecognized, and they may go unrecognized by whole communities or societies. We need to be careful with the use of the notion of recognition, since it can have a connotation of detecting. Moral judgment is not a kind of detection, if detection implies that there is an object waiting for discovery. It is perfectly all right to say that we can recognize the wrongness of cruelty or to say that someone does not recognize the wrongness of what she has done. But recognitions of this kind are more like recognizing the architecture as Georgian than it is like recognizing one's hat at the lost-and-found office or the color as scarlet and not pink. This is not to say that these judgments are inferential. But they involve, or are at least supported by, explanatorily relevant discriminations that may involve fairly textured conceptual articulation. And additional articulation can enable us to make recognitions we were not capable of previously, and as a result we can appreciate prescriptive significance that did not figure in our reasoning before.

A situation can admit of more than one ethical description. This is what happens in cases of incommensurability, where different descriptions yielding different reasons are warranted and it is not the case that one is more correct than the other. As a result, we might find ourselves acknowledging the force of reasons pulling us in incompatible directions. For example, a situation may be such that we cannot both satisfy standards of loyalty to a friend and standards of fairness. Moral realism is not, as such, committed to total commensurability, and practical reasoning, as such, need not lead to a single best choice. Just as theoretical reasoning may reveal that the world is heterogeneous, that there is not one true theory of it all, practical reasoning may reveal that ethical value cannot be reductively interpreted. There is no a priori reason to think that there is one fundamental, contentful criterion of value. Good, like truth, may be manifold. There are many truths (biological truths, physical truths, psychological truths), and there may be varieties of ethical good (courage is not good in just the same way that loyalty is). Incommensurability of goods, when it occurs, is not indicative of incoherence. Whether there is incommensurability or not is a matter of what the facts are. Moral theory is often conceived as though it were a kind of grid of criteria that, when imposed upon the world, will yield clear and definite courses of action or rankings of them. We should instead conceive of it as arising out of consideration of the world and responsive to the texture and heterogeneity of the considerations it presents. If multiple descriptions are merited, this need not be because of the influence of subjectivity. It may well be because of the complexity and nonreducibility of what is found.

Some people are much better describers than others; they notice more detail and more relations, and their descriptions better express the complexity of the phenomena. And describing is often explanatory, not just a listing of features. We can describe how someone plays tennis in a way that reveals her strategy, her employment of her skills, and view of the game. We can describe the construction of a railroad station in terms that refer to projected traffic loads, expectations of future mixes of passenger and freight use, and so forth. A good describer of a tennis match understands and expresses what is going on through a grasp of what makes for tennis and can judge the play through a grasp of what makes for skilled play. A good ethical describer of the features of a situation similarly understands and expresses their relevance to judgment and action and sees what they count for. Description can be a good deal more than reporting, and ethically relevant description surely is. It may involve grasping someone else's motives, recognizing the case as precedent-setting, anticipating someone else's feelings being hurt, and the like.

A good deal of learning ethical concepts and learning how to reason about ethical matters turns on becoming more perceptive and thorough in describing the ethically relevant aspects of people and situations. A description can be unambitious or lazy, in the sense that it simplifies the ethical character of its object or ignores aspects of it that constitute considerations of a sort one is blind to or does not wish to entertain or reveal. If we are using practical reason in an articulate, attentive way, the ethical dimensions of what is being described will be captured and expressed in the description. It will reveal what are the relevant ethical considerations. They may be ambiguous or heterogeneous or fail to point to a single correct judgment or course of action. But ethical understanding is reflected in description, in characterizing motives, in identifying attitudes, in recognizing harms and their causes and so on. In arguing about what ethically matters in a situation or in trying to decide what to do or how to react, we are in part trying to figure out what description is ethically accurate. That is how we recognize facts as counting as reasons, as having weight for judgment and decision.

For example, we might be unmoved by someone's difficult circumstances because the difficulty does not involve us and we do not have any emotional stake in it. Then, when something similar happens to someone we do care strongly about, our appreciation of that sort of difficulty changes. It changes not just emotionally; we redescribe it because our interest and desire to understand it more fully are engaged. We find that the enhanced understanding and description also apply to the first instance, and many of the same considerations for acting in certain ways obtain because of the similarity of the facts. We thus realize the generality of those considerations and the comparability of weight that they have across persons. In a case of this sort, it is not our attitudinal response that makes for the ethical significance; rather, it serves to prompt what would have been the right understanding prior to our change in attitude.

The kind of attention that makes for good ethical description entails exercising practical reason responsibly. As an example of exercising reason responsibly as a form of attention, consider what is involved in reading and mastering a text, as opposed to reading it just to pass the time or for recreation. In the former case we strive to grasp the overall argument or thrust of it; we attend to fine points and connect up this text with the rest of our understanding of the issues. We might go back over it, realizing that second and third looks may alter our understanding and appreciation of it. We want to be able to explicate it to others, or at least discuss and criticize it in an informed manner. Some of the same kinds of cognitive exertion are employed in achieving understandings with practical reason. If we are responsible, we react to situations and deliberate about them with rational concern, concern to find an illuminating, accurate description of the ethical significance of the facts. We want to appreciate them in a way that fits into a larger, textured ethical understanding. We may find that our understanding motivates us to revise our policies of judgment and action or that it squares with them, giving us confidence in their soundness. Part of being ethically responsible is this sort of concern to see what ethically matters, without bias and the distortions of self-centeredness or succumbing to passions.

When we say, "Yes, that is a good reason to help him this time, but next time he's on his own," this use of "good" is descriptive in a practical sense, and its appropriateness depends upon the facts. Similarly with a statement such as "*That* sort of thing is not helpful in these circumstances," where what is meant is perhaps that it is likely to cause resentment or it is unfair or unkind. A person with practical wisdom is someone who reliably makes correct practical judgments because they have the appropriate understanding. A judgment that doing x to someone will cause them pain is a causal judgment. A judgment that pain caused like that is gratuitous, undeserved, or mean-spirited indicates ethical articulation and is a ground for taking it to be wrongful. The causal situation and its ethical significance are factual matters, and in identifying something as wrong or compassionate, we are descriptively registering what practical reason recognizes in them.

METAETHICS MATTERS

One might claim that it is possible to remain skeptical about practical realism, in a Humean spirit deny that this undermines ethics, and assert that it only undermines inflated claims about it. In this view, ethics, like our thinking about causality, can remain in place without realist support being found for it. But the issue is not that tractable. Projectivist prescriptivity naturalizes ethics in that it grounds norms in habits and policies of response and interest that themselves are not products of cognition. But practical reason in its ethical employment is not explicable by a naturalism of this type. Practical reason's prescriptivity is neither autonomous (as Kant held it was) nor derivative (as in a Humean account). What makes it practical is that it has a telos; it is reason that aims at what is good in the sense of both taking good as its object and having the realization of good as its aim. What makes it reason is that it can be informed by factual understanding. If it were not so informed, it would be a capacity that is causally relevant to action but not prescriptively relevant. It would not be a power to acknowledge and comprehend anything counting as reason-giving or reason-making for a purposive being that acts under concepts.

Realists, antirealists, and people who think the debate is unimportant to ethics can all agree that people have moral beliefs and can agree that when they say that something is wrong or obligatory, and so forth, they are not doing nothing but emotively expressing themselves. Mackie, for example, employs an error-theory in order to explain how, even though there are multiple sources for an impetus to objectification, there are no objective values and there is no objective prescriptivity. A strength of this approach is that it does not explain away these sources of objectification by linguistic or conceptual analysis. At the first-order level, it seems to leave them pretty much alone. But Mackie insists throughout that it is not objective considerations that credential any substantive practical principles. At the second-order level objectification is, he believes, revealed to be a constellation of errors. This could destabilize ethics, in a way, if we regard exposure of our "error" as requiring a revision in what we take first-order practice to amount to[50] (though it is not clear that it would). Mackie, however, does not explore this. But his account rests on a fairly narrow interpretation of objectivity. It seems to countenance Platonism and Kantianism as its models, rather than as two possible versions among others.

This chapter has offered a conception of moral objectivity that is neither Platonist nor Kantian, nor vulnerable to the main charges against naturalistic supervenience theories. The approach is intended to provide an answer to the question what sort of rational responsibility moral claims can and should live up to. Practical realism is a naturalistic metaethic, one that purports to account for both the cognitive dimension and the motivational dimension of moral claims.

The mobilization of attitudes and stances into ethical commitments and claims that are endorsable after critical scrutiny requires us to acknowledge that those claims not only figure importantly in life and action but are about something. They are not about moral facts, if that means finding and reporting an additional aspect of how things are. Facts are moral considerations for reason, which is practical, and there is such a thing as practical truth (though, again, moral realism need not be committed to there being unique, correct answers to all moral questions). Truths for practical reason are truths *of* practical reason; their being truths with prescriptive import depends upon their being included in a practical comprehension. But the facts that are so included are the plain old facts, realistically interpreted. They are morally significant for reason having a practical telos and thinking in terms of worth, point, and good.

What often seems wrong or inappropriate about moral realism is that it would have moral thought be too much like theoretical thought and understates significant differences. What often seems wrong with antirealism is that it does not leave enough space for understanding, explanation, and justification in moral thought. If we recognize human reason to be practical, then we can see how moral values, thought, and claims can be interpreted realistically. This answers to a need of practical reason to have an object and to the need of practical reason's understanding to be prescriptive.

CHAPTER 2

From Metaethics to Moral Psychology

This chapter is short and transitional. Having set out some programmatic considerations about metaethics and practical reason, we are almost ready to take up the topics in moral psychology. Before doing so, however, it will be useful to speak about character, its formation, and its relation to practical reason and thus bring the discussion, which has so far been fairly abstract, closer to the level of concreteness found in the remaining chapters. The focus here is on the broadly naturalistic dimensions of Aristotle's conceptions of character and self-determination. These conceptions will be, in the main, defended, though with some revision.

It should be observed at the beginning of the discussion of moral psychology that it might seem that these topics have no special tie to realism. A critic of realism might agree with the realist on the significance of self-love, friendship, and respect but deny that realist metaethics has anything to add to our understanding of them. Or even if the critic disagrees with the substantive claims about these topics, he might deny that the disagreement has anything to do with the merits of realism or antirealism. I shall try to show that realist considerations are part of our best account of these issues and that realism is not just ornamental with regard to them.

What is at stake in moral psychology is the general theory of the individual who participates in morality. If the individual's moral engagement with the world is correctly explicated as a realist one, that matters. It matters because exploration of topics in moral psychology will reveal how cognition of moral significance makes the individual a certain sort of person. If it is true that how we understand is determinative of the correctness of our ethical judgments, and these shape our commitments and dispositions and practices, then there is an important sense in which character is shaped by cognitive engagement with the world. Moral psychology and how the world is are not altogether independent of each other. To put the point in a somewhat exaggerated form, as practical beings, we are what we think good. And if the defense of practical realism succeeds, then it is plainly crucial that we think rightly about what is good. Antirealists will claim that what we think good is a matter of what we are, what we are in terms of our desires, sensibility, and propensities. I have argued that even these are not independent of reason in a human being. Claims about how desires and affective responses properly figure ethically are claims of practical reason. What is practically rational does not simply "follow" something nonrational. So there is a role for realism in moral psychology. Its role is to facilitate explanations of why and how certain convictions, forms of regard, attitudes, needs, and ideals are morally credentialed or warranted. It has a role in explaining what makes for good character.

CHARACTER, REASON, AND HABITUATION

According to Aristotle, the content and organization of character are brought about through processes that are in a broad sense naturalistic. They are not deterministic or mechanistic, but they are processes that occur in and through one's choices, experiences, emotions, what one is taught to fear, expected to do and to want, and so forth. Human beings have capacities for reflection upon, and criticism and revision of, emotions, judgments of worth, purposes, motives, and so on. The individual's character is not merely a product of social forces or merely a product of the working out of a natural program. But our rationality is the rationality of human beings, of animals with a certain kind of constitution and certain kinds of innate abilities. The development of character is not a process that simply happens in us or is imposed. We have a causal role in the formation of our own character, and it is the capacity for practical reasoning that is the ground of that causality.

In book 10 of the *Ethics* Aristotle again takes up one of the issues that he opened with, namely, how we come to have good character: "Now some think that we are made good by nature, others by habituation, others by teaching" (*N.E.* 1179b 20). He then indicates how each of the three has a role. Some people are fortunate in their natural tendencies. These do not fully determine character, but an element of natural endowment is surely present and important. This is, I think, particularly clear with respect to a characteristic such as temperance. Someone might just have moderate appetites and not find that he or she has to struggle to control or regulate them. This is not to say they are simply good by nature, but having moderate propensities makes the handling of the appetites easier. Similarly, some people are naturally more physically courageous than others, are less quick to become angry, or find it easier to extend their sympathies. It is very difficult to ascertain to what extent such things are innate and to what extent learned. But it is plain that there is variability in natural endowment with respect to them.

The issue of habituation is complex. This is not simply the stamping of dispositions onto someone. While young children do not deliberate (at least, not much) and do not have guiding conceptions of good action, they are still voluntary agents. Being habituated involves luck to the extent that one may be habituated well or badly. But as reason matures and is (or can be expected to be) exercised, the degree of responsibility for one's character increases. Aristotle's claim that "now not to know that it is from the exercise of activities on particular objects that states of character are produced is the mark of a thoroughly senseless person" (*N.E.* 1114a 10) is an extremely important part of his account of character, and one with a solid grain of truth in it. One of the things reason and experience enable us to understand is that if we engage in a certain kind of activity in a certain way, it can become a policy of action, a settled disposition to do that sort of thing from a certain kind of motive. Habit supplies starting points and dispositional momentum. But there remains plasticity in character, and it is shaped and oriented by our own deliberate actions. If we already desire and take pleasure in good acts, then coming to have good character is easier. But having habits does not neutralize the efficacy of deliberate action to shape character. Being rational and capable of criticism and valuation, we are capable of partially causing our own character by our judgments and actions. We can, to an extent, choose what to be committed to, control what we think good, and exert ourselves to be this or that sort of person. We can attend to facts and experiences and feelings and motives, and we can educate our sensibility and inform our character by reasoned consideration and choice. We can not just decide to have a certain character. But we can make decisions and perform actions that cause us to have certain characteristics.

Sometimes an effort of will is aimed not just at performing this or that action but at trying to alter our dispositions, trying to establish some policy of action or response as second nature. We can recognize that there is a difference between a good time and a good action, and we can make the discrimination on the basis of understanding. Even feelings can be influenced by judgment and choice. We can recognize that our feelings are of the wrong sort (too vindictive, too defensive, too hard, for example) and, through our appreciation of what would be better responses and motives, alter our feelings. This is not something we can do by simple decision, but it is something we can do by choosing to act differently. Through getting himself to act differently, a person can modify the feeling that is part of the action. If someone makes an effort to stop gossiping, he or she may, as a result, lose the appetite for it. Or if someone comes to recognize that putting others down really isn't a decent and fair thing to do, it may cease to be enjoyable, and the motive toward it will be drained. A feeling is not chosen, but we can choose to perform the kinds of actions that, if performed regularly, will cause us to have a changed affective disposition.[1]

On teaching, Aristotle says that we can not argue people into being good or make them good by teaching them theory. But argument does "seem to have power to encourage and stimulate the generous-minded among our youth, and to make a character which is gently born, and a true lover of what is noble, ready to be possessed by virtue" (*N.E.* 1179b 6–9). Argument is not, he says, efficacious with the many. Two things should be said about this. First, people with good starting points can be encouraged and stimulated by argument and discussion. They may well appreciate it and be improved by it. Second, to have good starting points, we need not be gently born or a lover of what is noble. That is, we do not need a conception of what is noble or fine that is strictly Aristotelian in form or content in order to have a contentful conception of human goods and needs. We just said that variability in natural propensities is important, and here's a place to see how. Given his propensities, a person may be more or less easy to habituate well, and as he matures, more or less responsive to reason. Many people, exhibiting a fairly wide range of backgrounds and early socialization, can, through teaching, encouragement, and others' taking their soundness of character seriously, come to take it seriously themselves. This is one place where Aristotle's account is too constricted and too confined to a certain group of people. If by "gently born, and a true lover of what is noble" Aristotle means that some people by natural endowment are more easily able to acquire the virtues, then his suggestion is very plausible. And those people will be more responsive to argument and discussion about ethical matters, and they will feel a personal stake in taking argument and discussion seriously. If what he means is that the potentiality for virtue is differentially present in different social classes of people, then we have reason to be skeptical of the observation.

Aristotle does, early on, put great weight on habit, but later (especially in books 2, 3, 6, and 9) gives an important role to reason. In fact, the textual order in which weight is put on these character-forming influences corresponds loosely to the order in which they actually have influence. He began with the discussion of habit and then went on to discuss deliberation and responsibility for character, and in book 6 presented the account of practical wisdom in his treatment of intellectual virtues. The moral virtues are virtues of the nonrational part of the soul but are virtues through being obedient to reason. They begin to be obedient through habituation to what other persons' practical reason directs, and then are obedient to the individual's own exercise of reason. There is, then, a role for reason throughout the development of character. In acquiring habits of choice and action, a person is developing a conception of good. This is how values are transmitted. A disposition to choose and act is also a disposition to value things in certain ways. Values come into view not by learning a theory of value but by enacting values, and the enactment (for good or ill) is originally undertaken as practice without understanding. The understanding, or, more neutrally, the conception, of what is good to do emerges from the practice. The individual with good habits is positioned to acquire practical knowledge.

As appetitive and passional beings, we seek direction and objects for our desires and passions. This direction and fixing of objects are formed in large part by practical interaction with and imitation of others. We seek to form a character; early on, the seeking is not self-conscious and is shaped by others. Later, it can be more deliberate and more knowing. But no one could originally form conceptions of good and be disposed to act on them just by thinking about them. Practical cognition needs to be *learned*. Dispositions can develop into dispositions to recognize, understand, and judge.

If we understand Aristotle's theory of action to involve agent causality, it is still a naturalistic power of agency that humans have, in the sense that we are authors of our actions through the exercise of natural capacities. Our capacities to deliberate, to make judgments of worth, and to act are not cut off from appetition and from features of character developed through habituation. They are not external to "empirical" character. The rationality that enables us to be agents develops and matures. A very young person is rational but not yet exercising deliberative, action-guiding rationality. As she matures, at the same time that habituation is forming dispositions, the individual is increasingly capable of critical appraisal of her own actions and motives and is increasingly capable of self-determination through deliberation. So one process, habituation, is establishing features of character through actions that are voluntary but not chosen through deliberation. Another process, that by which capacities for rational self-determination mature, enables individuals to be responsible authors of deliberate action and to consider and undertake to revise their own dispositions. Even at an early age, rationality is included in action, at least in the sense that young persons typically know what they are doing. It is not conditioning, if that is understood not to involve understanding. So the young person who has learned *that* certain ways of acting are right but does not know the *because* is acting from habit, but he is a rational individual acting from habit. He is progressively more and more capable of a critical appreciation of his own dispositions and the conceptions of good that they involve. The rationality that enables this critical appreciation also enables him to try to change his dispositions to be more in agreement with what, as he matures, he comes to understand.

This is not exactly what Aristotle says, but it is not fundamentally at odds with it, and it is a way of defusing what might appear as an inconsistency between the role he assigns to habituation and his attribution to people of responsibility for their character.[2] Aristotle's account of action does not fit neatly under the headings often found in formulations of the debate on free will versus determinism. Part of the reason for this is that it is a developmental account according to which deliberative capacities increase with maturity and experience. He is not, like Kant, concerned to mark off a sphere of free action by sequestering it from interference by empirical conditions. He is interested in articulating what sort of deliberative self-determination a human being can be reasonably expected to exhibit, given that some of what we do is plainly up to us and that how we act shapes our dispositions to act. There is no inconsistency between the role he assigns to habituation and his attribution of responsibility for character to people, as long as we recognize the developmental dynamic of rational action.

A rational animal can conceptualize its ends, evaluate them, and organize them into a way of living. And it is part of doing this rationally that they have some coherent mutual fit, even if they do not all converge on one final specific end, one specific good thing the individual aims to accomplish. Everyone (rationally) aims at the good in the sense that it is rational to choose ends and policies of action that are found to be desirable for their own sake. Different goods can be part of this conception, but a human being, on account of his nature, must lead a life structured by practical reasoning, which is inescapably valuational. This is the kind of causality essential to a human life. As I suggested earlier, much of the motion of a human being is rational motion. And this is not optional, and neither, then, is aiming at good.

Additionally, like other animals, a human being develops. He not only grows bodily with associated changes in physical capacities (e.g., locomotive, reproductive); he develops in terms of the maturation of his potentialities for rational motion, for deliberation, judgment, choice, and action. Early on, we naturally act primarily from appetite and habit. One way to interpret the role that Aristotle gives to habit is not that it fixes our character but that, early on, *of course* it is the formative factor because we're not yet able to employ practical reason. Its importance is not that it closes off the openness that reasoning affords us but it shapes dispositions to act, which are for a time the primary motivational factors and are not easily changed. But his discussion of habituation comes *after* he has introduced a central claim about human action, that it is aimed at some good, at a conception of good that is rationally articulable and striven for through rational means. Habit disposes but not does not necessitate, and it does not drive out rational action guided by conceptions of worth that the agent is responsible for.

Aristotle maintains that a sound character, a character constituted by the virtues, can become fixed and unchangeable, and so too can bad character. It is an important part of his view that character becomes fully established as a second nature and its plasticity diminishes virtually to zero. There is not a self or a will in addition to the character that can bring about changes in the latter or guide action contrary to its tendencies. As an agent, you simply are your character in action, actualizing what you take to be good, and there is no independent will, rational or otherwise, that is a source of agency. Being good and acting well are not a matter of acting contrary to one's character. This is why it is so important to Aristotle that character be well formed and that people take responsibility for their character. Moreover, we cannot tell in advance what difference an action or policy of action will make to our character.

> But actions and states of character are not voluntary in the same way; for we are masters of our actions from the beginning right to the end, if we know the particular facts, but though we control the beginning of our states of character the gradual progress is not obvious, any more than it is in illnesses; because it was in our power, however, to act in this way or not in this way, therefore the states are voluntary. (*N.E.* 1114b 30–35)

Our states of character are voluntary because the actions that cause us to have them are voluntary, even though much of that voluntary action is guided by habituation and not by mature deliberation. But voluntariness for Aristotle is a matter more of self-movement than of exercising a distinct power of willing, and so there is not the sort of conflict between causal necessitation and freedom of the will that is focal in so much modern theorizing.

Aristotle's line on the voluntariness of character is a hard one, and it does not take into account in a systematic way how poor upbringing or physiological or psychological abnormality or defect can be causal factors in explaining poor character. He does argue that upbringing is terribly important, but he does not excuse bad character on account of bad upbringing. The combination of voluntariness of action and what he takes to be a common ability to see that like actions lead to like dispositions grounds his claim for each person being responsible for his or her character.

We need, however, to make some allowances that Aristotle does not make. If one is habituated by and surrounded by people who are intemperate, unfair, and emotionally volatile, for example, this can in large part explain that person's having poor character, even though it does not make it inevitable. It is extremely difficult to separate out and measure causal factors such as natural temperament and propensities, the influence of other people and circumstances, and psychological variables. While the combination of these is not enough to erode our conviction that, in general, people have a good deal of responsibility for their character, what Aristotle takes as the norm involves more luck than he openly allows for. Sorabji discusses this issue:

> The difficult case is that of the man, who becomes bad by *heeding* his mentors, when they give him evil instruction. He too makes a contribution, but one he can hardly be blamed for, when he abides by what he was taught. Though Aristotle argues that standing by bad principles does not deserve credit (*N.E.* vii 2, 1146a 16–31, and vii 9), he cannot maintain that, in a case like this, it deserves blame. It is a pity that Aristotle does not consider more carefully whether a man can then be blamed for the eventual outcome: acquiring a bad character. The problem however, is not one about there being an external origin, with him contributing nothing; for he does contribute something. The question is rather one about whether he ever had a fair opportunity.[3]

On the one hand, texture needs to be added to Aristotle's account. It ignores causal factors that are real and significant. On the other hand, this texture is not at odds with the general sort of broadly naturalistic approach Aristotle takes. Free action is not just a matter of external liberty or absence of external constraint. Neither is it a matter of an autonomous inner act of willing distinct from the tendencies, propensities, and other content of character.

C. A. Campbell, for example, argues that

> from the inner standpoint, it seems to me plain, there is no difficulty whatever in attaching meaning to an act which is the self's act and which never the less does not follow from the self's character.[4]

And:

> What this implies—and it seems to me to be an implication of cardinal importance for any theory of the self that aims at being more than superficial—is that the nature of the self is for itself something more than just its character as so far formed. The "nature" of the self and what we commonly call the "character" of the self are by no means the same thing, and it is utterly vital that they should not be confused. The "nature" of the self comprehends, but is not without remainder reducible to, its "character"; it must, if we are to be true to the testimony of our experience of it, be taken as including *also* the authentic creative power of fashioning and refashioning "character."[5]

This isn't quite the Kantian dualism of rational personality and empirical character, but it still involves a distinction between the agency of the self and the causal tendencies of character. For all of the lack of needed texture in Aristotle's view, it has the advantage of comprising the causal powers of an individual's constitution in one complex of capacities, rather than dividing them into agent causality and empirical causality. What is crucial is not whether there is in us a kind of agency that can act contrary to our character but how we exercise the capacities that cause us to have a single, overall second nature that is character. These capacities include practical reason, but not as a power with nonnatural causality or with a distinct set of objects.

A capacity can be identified *by* its exercise but it is not to be identified with it. So there is a sense in which our character is somewhat plastic and we can exercise capacities in a way intended to change our character. This is what we do when we recognize some characteristic we wish not to have and are thereby motivated to change it. The change is a matter of pursuing a new policy of action, of acquiring a new habit, and cannot be brought about simply by decision or an act of will. It is not plausible that we have an established character but, when we need to, we can act contrary to it. Either one won't be able to act contrary to it, or doing so will alter this character. To say that there is a potentiality for alteration of character is not to be committed to an additional causal power.

There is an important symmetry in Aristotle's theory between good character and bad. Both can become fixed and unchangeable, and the virtuous individual and vicious individual act regularly and in accordance with choice according to their character. According to Aristotle, virtuous activity is durable, more durable even than scientific knowledge (*N.E.* 1100b 10–20). And happiness is durable as well, and not easily taken away (*N.E.* 1096b 25). Presumably, vices too, once established, are enduring and not easily changed, and persons who are unhappy on account of their vices may find it much easier to regret what they've made of themselves than to change themselves.

Here again Aristotle's line may be a bit too hard. It is not easy and it does not happen often, but one's character can change somewhat (for better or worse) even after it is mature and largely established. Persons of sound character leading choiceworthy lives recognize that the way they are supplies them with a reason to go on being that way. Persons who are unhappy because of dissatisfaction with their own character recognize a reason to try to change. The recognition and the trying count for something, even if the prospects for success are not great. It must be painful and disturbing to look upon one's life or character with regret and acknowledge that one has become like that through voluntary actions. In this sense, one has made oneself miserable voluntarily, though without having had misery as an end. People's character may be incorrigible in the sense that they just never take seriously the possibility that they have serious vices. While one's capacity for rationality does not diminish once character is firmly established, its manner of exercise and engagement with its objects is part of what is firmly established. Aristotle may well be right that a point is reached where a bad man cannot become good and an unhappy one happy. But there need not be some common definite point across persons. We should add, though, that it is difficult for the bad person to change because his practical understanding is defective and this is associated with dispositions of the emotions and appetites that by adulthood are generally quite firmly established. For the person of good character, not only are his dispositions also quite firmly established but he has and can understand reasons to go on in many of the ways he acts. The bad person may believe he, too, has good reasons to carry on as he has, but he will both be mistaken about this and have passional dispositions that cause him to persist in the error.

Current understanding of psychological disorder, addiction, neurosis, stress, and human physiology generally gives us reason to identify factors impinging on voluntariness that Aristotle did not recognize. This is not to say that one has one's character involuntarily, because, for whatever one is like, there is a causal story. Everyone has a story, but it is a story that includes a measure of authorship attributable to voluntariness. As he argued, we do not have good reason to explain both virtue and vice as involuntary or nonvoluntary, and we can not just excuse vice but credit people with their virtues.

There are general (but not exceptionless) norms of what can be expected of people, of what is up to them and how they are able to deliberate, choose, and act. And they are substantiated by a mass of human experience and by theorizing about human capacities. The strength of the Aristotelian view lies in its possibilities for explaining our values, concerns, and characteristics in terms of how we exercise capacities in voluntary action and of how these capacities include reasoning, the appetites, and the emotions in a unified repertoire of powers and susceptibilities constitutive of a human personality, rather than in separating out a conscience or a will or pure practical reason as an authority or agency distinct from character. Aristotle's notion of a specific function for human nature and his account of virtuous activity as that which enables us to realize our intrinsic end may be metaphysically optimistic, and it may give to voluntariness too straightforward a role in the fashioning of character. But what is needed is further qualification, an extended range of excusing conditions and an enhanced appreciation of the complexity of character, rather than a rejection of the general strategy of explanation.

Our understanding of what is important and of how to live is developed as we go along. Much of it is experimental, or at least exploratory, and is not a straightforward matter of carrying out a plan elaborated in advance. The good is not a target in the sense of a fixed object that we work our way toward (and along just one straight and narrow course). It makes sense to speak of it as a target insofar as acting well and leading a good life involve rationally organized activity, activity that is directed by understanding. It is not an accident that one lives well. It is something achieved by directed striving. But rules of good action and a plan for living well are consequent upon the particulars of action, experience, and circumstances and are not formulations from which the structure and character of a good life can be theoretically inferred. Practical knowledge is not only *about* practice; it *emerges* from it. While much of our practical reasoning and activity is concerned with pursuing what we take to be in our interests, a very important part of practical reasoning and activity figures in our finding out what our interests are. Nor is this just a matter of finding out what our deepest or strongest desires are. It is also a process of coming to new, differently informed and articulated conceptions of what is desirable. Both coming to know what is good for us and seeking it are, in a broad sense, naturalistic processes. They occur through action, experience, and a variety of types of human relations and interactions. Central to these processes is the cultivation (though in a nontheoretical way) of a sense of what is important, what is worth doing, what sort of person it is worth it to be and to be with. That is, central to them is the cultivation of an understanding of the world by practical reason, and this includes how to identify and describe what is ethically relevant and a grasp of how it counts with respect to action.

The education of practical reason is not a matter of our being able to bring a certain set of entities or properties into view. It is a matter of the teleology of practical reason being well ordered through the successively better informed exercise of it. At the same time, we don't even know what ethical problems might arise, and we may not have solutions to them, even if we knew the relevant ethical facts. That there are facts is a different matter from there being answers. It has been remarked several times that one respect in which this account differs from Aristotle's is in not including a specific intrinsic end for human nature. That there is no such end, or that we do not have a satisfactory conception of what it might be, makes ethics harder. In a sense, at the very center of practical thought is the fact that human beings have to figure out how to live. We work out ways to live, and some of them are quite excellent and admirable, others not. But there is no formula or plan for a best form of personal or social life or both, except in the very general sense that it is good to be guided by an understanding of the ethical significance of facts. That is, it is good to have, and to act in conformity with, knowledge of human goods, needs, and interests. It is rational to desire an understanding of value and to organize one's desires and motives by that understanding. That is a way of being good, and of being good to ourselves in large part by being true to our nature. Ethics concerns what it is intrinsically good to do, even if there is no comprehensive target—a good or best life overall—that practical activity aims at. It is a good for the individual to be good; it is the basis of proper self-love and self-respect. In that regard, ethical goodness is a central feature of a good life. But there need not be an end of all we do, a superordinate end to which all others are subordinate or of which all activities are partially constitutive, in order for there to be real goods for the teleology of practical reasoning.

COGNITIVISM AND CHARACTER

An important feature of habituation is the learning of ethical description: how to understand it and how to give it. Habituation entails not just the development of patterns of desire and emotion but also skills of perception, recognition, and articulation. If a young person is trained in habits of patience, consideration of others, honesty, and so forth, she will likely also be better able to identify them in others. Habits not only shape dispositions understood as determinants of behavior; they can also involve the shaping of abilities to notice and appreciate kinds of things. Bad habits may very well result in one's ethical attention and their repertoire of recognitional and descriptive abilities being misguided. Reasoning and reason giving are themselves in large part learned by habituation. Not only motives or appetitive tendencies are established by habit; the vocabulary of description, the idiom of attention and perception are also learned. Habituation is not only a nonrational predecessor to reasoning. It is how practical reason is initially educated, and it is a condition for it maturing and for the individual having an interest in being able to understand and act for good reasons.

In this respect, ethical understanding is both naturalistic and rationalist; that is, it is developed in a broadly naturalistic way, but what is developed is rational understanding. How we come to be sound or unsound practical reasoners depends in large part upon how we learn practices of judgment and acquire emotive and motivational dispositions. But the habits that are formed are not blind. They can be rational habits, habits of attention, reasoning, and judgment. Even where our responses are emotionally charged or emotionally motivated, they can be rational and can express more than emotion. Responses of revulsion, feelings of gratitude, anger, indignation, compassion, and so forth, are not independent of reason or necessarily impediments to it. They can reflect understanding as well as affect.

So much of the debate in moral philosophy has cast cognitivism versus noncognitivism in a certain way so that it is easy to think of habits as fundamentally nonrational dispositions of desire or emotion in contrast to knowledge, which includes reason, justification, and the resources of logic and evidence. But a habit need not be independent of reason. It can both involve reason and be justified or appraised on the basis of rational considerations. A person can be habituated in, among other things, a sense of what is important, which is not, in the final analysis, a matter only of desire. To have a sense that x is important is to want to do it, have it, bring it about, or see it done. But our sense of what is important concerns what we take there to be good reasons for; and that sense can be tested and judged on the basis of the understanding embedded in and exhibited by it. It involves awareness, discrimination, and an articulation of what is choiceworthy. It is inculcated without objective, theoretical self-consciousness. But in a rational being it can be cognitively criticized, revised, and appraised. That is, it can be responsive to the determinations of practical reason, where it is not simply ushering passion into action, showing the way with a bit of logic and causal information. Practical cognition can itself be motivational, not without desires or sensibility but by informing them in such a way that they figure as commitments concerning what is good or choiceworthy. For people whose wants and interests are responsive to their understanding, the premises of their practical reasoning are not in any explanatorily useful sense supplied from origins that are noncognitive. Such a person wants to have sound practical understanding, and her wants are regulated by her understanding. It is in this sense that a conception of what it is good to do need not be driven by what is essentially noncognitive.[6]

CHAPTER 3

Self-love

In this and the next two chapters a number of topics in moral psychology will be discussed. These chapters are meant to develop the realism and the conception of practical reason already laid out, to lend concreteness to the more abstract considerations that came earlier, and to illustrate their relevance and explanatory role. Much of this account is articulation and reconstruction of some of Aristotle's views, not primarily as exegesis but because they are so apt as resources for this type of realism and its associated conception of the role of practical reason in understanding ethical value and as a cause of action and a certain kind of enjoyment concomitant to good action.

SELF-LOVE AND HUMAN NATURE

Human beings are capable of self-love, and they need it. They can think of their lives as worthwhile and can enjoy not just this or that, but enjoy leading a life. This is not self-love in the sense of egoism, as it is generally understood. It is not a matter of putting one's own interests or desires first or of thinking that because an interest or desire is one's own, it carries weight that those of others don't carry. I will argue in this chapter that self-love of a certain kind is possible for us because we are rational and that it is a good of the first rank. Practical reason is not just a means of pursuing one's interests; certain exercises of it are constitutive causes of self-love, and self-love so caused is desirable in itself. Machines are not capable of self-love, and neither are nonrational animals. The judgment that going on in a certain way, that leading *this* kind of life, is worthwhile is a judgment of reason. Being able to make this judgment, and to make it truly without self-deception, is one of a human being's most prized achievements. The idea here is that the informed exercise of practical reason is something we enjoy. The exercise of practical reason not only is what enables us to act well, it also causes us to enjoy doing so. What is enjoyed is acting in accordance with a true conception of what is good. This is practical self-knowledge, insofar as what is good for us depends upon our nature. This is not to say that ethically sound action is always to the individual's advantage. But the achievement of self-love and its worth are not matters of private advantage. They are matters of appreciating acting and living in ways that reason endorses.

It may seem that in order to be a self-lover in this sense, one must already be a self-lover in a different sense. One must already have the kinds of concern for one's character and activities that will make possible the achievement of self-love. That is true. Self-love is not achieved accidentally or just by willing it. It is achieved through policies of valuing, choosing, and acting, and a person must learn these through habituation, experience, and a modicum of reflection. In this way self-love is comparable to virtue. One must be trained in it in order to achieve it; a disposition to it must be established before it is up and running through one's own self-determination and understanding. Self-love, then, is something one succeeds at; it is a concomitant of certain kinds of activities one chooses. It is also something one needs. Lack of self-love is painful. To lack a sense of the worth of one's projects and activities is undermining. The goods we aim at, actualize, and are concerned with are not just goods for ourselves or goods of ourselves. But an appreciation of oneself as a locus of good activity is a condition for being at home in the world, of not being alienated from it and from other people. When one lacks self-love, the world is not appreciated as a setting in which one's activity counts as worthwhile. Nonrational beings do not need self-love because they do not act on conceptions of good and they cannot think of their agency as a cause of their own state. But a rational animal nonoptionally acts so and cannot, except pathologically, fail to appreciate itself as an agent whose activity makes a difference to its leading a life. We turn now to the account of self-love, and the moral psychology that supplies its context.

THE NORMATIVE NATURE OF SELF-LOVE

To a large extent, Aristotle's ethical theory is, or at least centrally concerns, a theory of causality. His ethics is a theory of the sort of causality exercised by a substance of a certain kind, a rational animal, actualizing its distinctive nature. A rationally well-ordered person is someone whose action is guided by understanding. Moral psychology, for Aristotle, is intimately bound up with metaphysics and philosophy of mind. Living well is consequent upon having a rationally organized soul. And that is a soul whose activity is shaped by a grasp of right ends and correct means to realize them. We need to know about the world and our own nature in order to understand what is involved in living well, in order to engage our causality to its proper objects.

In the enlarged literature on virtue in the last three or so decades, much of the focus has been on analyses of specific virtues, contrasts with deontological and utilitarian approaches to ethics, and also on the relation of virtues to objective considerations about human nature. The emphasis here is on the causality of practical reason, how it enables us to achieve conceptions of ethical good and moves us to act from those conceptions. This is not an endorsement of a particular version of virtue-ethics but an endorsement of elements of the picture of practical reason utilized in that approach.

Aristotle put a great deal of emphasis on habit and its role in forming character and governing action. He had the sound good sense not to mistake what is entailed by good action with the individual being able to produce a theoretical account of it. Reflection upon action and its qualities, however, reveals good action to be that which is explicable with reference to the truth, truth about human nature and people's situations. The moral virtues are constitutive and symptomatic of the causality of practical reason taking as its object the truth about what is good, given the human constitution. This view is plausible, for the reasons explored in the previous chapters.

Neither self-love nor friendship, in the primary sense, is a passion; they are kinds of active concern with associated sensibility importantly related to practical reason. Through the practical exercise of reason, we can understand human goods, aim at them, realize them, and in doing so succeed in knowing and enjoying our nature. What friendship and self-love, in their primary senses, both crucially involve is appreciation of a person as a locus of good activity. And this appreciation has realist bases, grounds in facts about human nature. In friendship and self-love we love persons as causes of and as instances of human good.

This last claim will figure especially prominently in the account. There are several ways in which Aristotle's account is incomplete or in need of revision. As the discussion proceeds, it will be clear how his views are being modified or departed from. There are, however, three elements of his discussion that surely are correct and profoundly important. First, self-love is crucially related to our *human* nature. Second, it is a *normative* matter. There is a genuine difference between justified and unjustified self-love. This may sound implausible because, after all, does not it seem that the evaluation of oneself, perhaps above anything, is a personal, subjective affair? This is one of the errors that Aristotle's view helps correct. Both self-love and friendship entail an understanding and appreciation of the *worth* of individuals. And this is, in respects we will explore, a matter about which one can judge well or badly, with knowledge or in error or ignorance. Third, there are fundamental causal relations between friendship and self-love. Aristotle argues that friendship is, in a way, an extension of self-love and that a friend is like another self. There is truth in this, but it is too one-sided. I will argue that the causal traffic flows both ways and that friendship is needed for self-love. To put the point simply, one cannot achieve self-love alone. It is not a private matter.

When I say that in both friendship and self-love we love persons as instances and causes of human good, I do not mean that there is just one kind of realization of human good. The best kinds of self-love and friendship are not restricted to persons with only certain excellences in a certain balance. We can be more pluralistic than Aristotle, while still recognizing that proper self-love and the better kinds of friendship imply acknowledgments of human worth and active appreciation of them. This is where the varieties of human character and social forms make a difference, without undercutting the objectivity of the relevant ethical considerations. For some people, self-knowledge and self-love may be achieved through a religiously oriented life. For others, they may come through political activity, through devotion to the arts, or through a number of other ways. But whatever one's personal commitments, special passions, or concerns, there are certain general characteristics of practical understanding and action that are fundamental to self-love. Surely there are "mixed" lives, lives involving commitments to a variety of ends and concerns, and there is no reason to think that one or another is *the* primary end or concern. While it is rational to have a coherent life-plan, coherence needn't involve singlemindedness or the assignment of overridingness to a particular element of the plan. Moreover, acting well, acting from practical reason's understanding of the ethical significance of facts, does not presuppose or imply that the agent lives a best kind of life. The significance of the facts explains what is good action, but it doesn't converge on a conception of a best life.

The bases of self-love include the causality of the agent in her being concerned for and doing things she judges to be worth doing, and in being correct about these matters. Certainly, if a person does something awful or disgusting, this is not properly a ground or support for self-love, and neither is leading a life of idle amusement or vindictive resentment or sycophantic dependency. When we recognize ways in which people go wrong or delude themselves or live a lie, it can become clearer how seriously we can and should take the idea of there being genuine human goods, needs, and interests, even if not a fixed list of them, each with a fixed weight.

Additionally, self-love is not egoistic or self-centered. A great deal of moral theorizing concerns the issue whether self-interest conflicts with moral considerations and whether and how it can be restrained by them or overridden by them. Part of what I hope to show is that self-love, in its proper sense, requires ethically sound character and is not mainly a matter of success at self-interested pursuits.

PLEASURE AND GOOD

As a way deeper into the topic, we need to look briefly at some of the elements of Aristotle's conception of mind and action, with a focus on pleasure.

Pleasure is not some single undifferentiated state that we aim at in order to maximize its degree and duration. Rather, it is a concomitant of activity. Aristotle is not as clear as we would like about this, but the central claim is not in doubt.

> Since every sense is active in relation to its object, and a sense which is in good condition acts perfectly in relation to the most

> beautiful of its objects (for perfect activity seems to be ideally of this nature: whether we say that it is active, or the organ in which it resides, may be assumed to be immaterial), it follows that in the case of each sense the best activity is that of the best-conditioned organ in relation to the finest of its objects. And this activity will be the most complete and pleasant. For, while there is pleasure in respect of any sense, and in respect of thought and contemplation no less, the most complete is pleasantest, and that of a well conditioned organ in relation to the worthiest of its objects is the most complete; and the pleasure completes the activity. (*N.E.* 1174b 15–24)

There are a number of points here relevant to the understanding of friendship and self-love, and, for that matter, virtue and rational activity generally. Pleasures are specific to the activities of different senses, or to the operation of different powers. Pleasure is not just one thing. Also, pleasures are qualitatively correlated with their objects. The senses, and reason too, have proper objects, and the pleasures that accompany engagement with these objects are qualitatively differentiated. "The pleasure proper to a worthy activity is good and that proper to an unworthy activity bad; just as the appetites for noble objects are laudable, those for base objects culpable" (*N.E.* 1175b 24–30). We can find pleasure in engagement with improper objects, for example, in being gleefully cruel or in being self-indulgently intemperate. It is not the case that weakness or vice is always painful but, rather, that the pleasure in them is bad pleasure. Pleasure completes or perfects activity, and since we aim at our activities being pleasurable, it is crucial that we aim at the right pleasures. We aim at what appears good to us, its appearance depending upon our character. "But in all such matters that which appears to the good man is thought to be really so. If this is correct, as it seems to be, and virtue and the good man as such are the measure of each thing, those will also be pleasures which appear so to him and those things pleasant which he enjoys" (*N.E.* 1176 a 14–19). And "to each man the activity in accordance with his own disposition is most desirable, and therefore, to the good man that which is in accordance with virtue" (*N.E.* 1176 b 25–27).

Thus, a further crucial point is that not only is pleasure a completion of activity and differentially correlated with different activities, but our own character also has a causal role in determining what we find pleasurable. While we all aim at pleasure, this is not to say that we are or should be hedonists. Pleasure as such is not what constitutes good for rational animals. There are criteria for evaluating pleasure that are based upon an understanding of what contributes to and constitutes a good life. As Julia Annas has stated:

> One's notion of what is pleasant is not external to one's conception of the good life; and the truly good life involves a notion of pleasure that is essentially connected to the performance of virtuous activities. So the good life and the truly pleasant life must be explained in terms of one another. What is rejected is a notion of pleasure as an end that is common to good and bad and with equal appeal to both. Goodness does not consist in avoiding pleasure in the interests of some higher ideal but in being right about what is truly pleasant.[1]

The importance of this is not just that we need reason to know and enjoy what is good but that the activity of reason is itself pleasurable, part of and not just a means to pleasure. I would add that in enjoying the right objects of activity, in exercising our powers in accordance with understanding, we enjoy our *selves*, i.e., we find being the individuals we are, leading the lives we lead, desirable for its own sake. A rationally well-ordered individual enjoys acting well.

Aristotle says that pleasure is that by which "the soul as a whole is consciously brought into its normal state of being" (*Rhetoric* 1370a 1–2) and that "it must therefore be pleasant as a rule to move towards a natural state of being, particularly when a natural process has achieved the complete recovery of that natural state" (1370a 3–5). In the first passage, "normal" surely does not refer to a statistical norm; "normal" is a notion of being in a good state. So, too, is the notion of a natural state. When we are talking about a person and her characteristics and activities, the normal state is not the typical one, or the one most often found, but the state of excellence. In that sense, virtue brings us into and maintains us in a normal state. And virtuous activity is pleasant because it is activity that realizes our good. Such activity is desirable for its own sake and is pleasurable in its being appreciated as good. There are a couple of points here we need to explore. One is that pleasure, or at least the pleasure of ethical virtue, is not a feeling, not a sensation. Another is that this pleasure is a concomitant of good activity.

One of the strengths of Aristotle's discussion of pleasure is that he interprets it as an activity or as supervenient upon activity, rather than as a psychic state in the more familiar empiricist sense. Because pleasure is consequent upon the well-functioning of a capacity, it is explained in terms of that capacity realizing a good, rather than good being explained in terms of pleasure. As incomplete as Aristotle's account is, it spares us the sort of muddle Mill got into in taking pleasure as what is good (because desirable for its own sake) and then trying to figure out which pleasures were better than others by checking people's preferences, given that they had wider rather than narrower experience.

In fact, it would seem, on Aristotelian lines, that some of the richest and most important kinds of pleasure do not "feel" like anything at all. When, for example, we are in good health, we say that we feel fine, but there is no particular sensation of this, no particular phenomenological feel to it. The normal or natural state of biological health is a good, and a good realized by physiological activity, but while it is pleasurable, it is not experienced as a psychic state or impression. Recovering from injury or disease is pleasurable, but it, too, involves no pleasure in anything like an occurrent feeling. Loss of a capacity, or a defect in it, may be painful as felt pain, or it may be painful just in the sense that it is bad to be in that condition, it is deprivation of a good. Such things as glaucoma, ulcers, or arthritis illustrate this. Even if one is not hurting, one's condition may be unpleasant because it is not normal, not achieving or maintaining the excellences of one's biological nature.

There are analogies here to the context of character. It is pleasurable and desirable for its own sake to exercise ethical virtues, though this is not because of a particular kind of affect. A virtue is an excellence of a realized capacity; it is a condition that enables a human being to be the cause of his own good. The exercise of it is pleasurable in that good action is desirable for its own sake and spares the agent the pain of internal conflict or regret. The good person loves being good but doesn't love it on account of its being a particular feeling he desired to bring about. The sort of pleasure involved here is more a matter of appreciation than of sensation.

Additionally, ethical virtues bring one into and maintain one in his normal state. The normal state of a rational animal is to be engaged in activity guided by correct understanding. Virtues of character order nonrational capacities to be in agreement with reason and enable one to realize his own good by doing what is good. It is desirable for its own sake and, in that sense, pleasurable to exercise the virtues, because in doing so one simply is in his natural or normal state.

"Natural" here refers to an ideal appropriate to the constitution of a human being. It does not refer to the potentialities for change of the sort Aristotle attributed to nature in the *Physics*. Still, the two notions are not unrelated. Given a being's nature (in the sense of its constitution, its potentialities, and its limits), there are goods appropriate to it, brought about by its own activity and representing success at realizing its nature. The completed state of success, or, rather, the ongoing activity that maintains the being in that state, is what is natural or normal for it.

For a human being, the activity that brings it into and maintains it in its normal state is rational activity. So, the principle of change and motion is not simply like that in other kinds of natural beings. In a sense, rational actions are not natural proceedings. But they are not nonnatural either. A human being has a rational soul, and it is the soul of a living, perceiving, acting animal. The main difference between human and nonhuman natural beings is that a human's activity of realizing his or her good is activity informed by understanding. It is a process of self-determination. Successfully leading a human life is not a natural process if by "natural" we mean "what goes on anyway, independent of judgment and choice." But leading such a life *is* natural in the sense that it centrally involves the individual exercising his or her constitutive capacities. Habit and action guided by practical knowledge are pleasing, and are so because of their role in bringing someone into his or her normal state. The individual with excellences of character and practical wisdom does not suffer the pain of internal conflict or the pain of shame or regret. Feeling fear is painful, and there are things even the courageous person is fearful of. Moreover, doing what courage requires may be painful. "Hence also courage involves pain, and is justly praised; for it is harder to face what is painful than to abstain from what is pleasant" (*N.E.* 1117a 33–35). So, virtuous activity can, of course, be attended by pain. But "the end which courage sets before it would seem to be pleasant" (*N.E.* 1117a 35). It is pleasurable to act nobly and to know that one's action is ethically sound. The cost in pain to a brave person is not a reason for her not to appreciate her virtue. A virtuous life is not a pain-free life, or a life chosen because it promises more pleasure than pain. It is a pleasurable life because of the desirability of the activities that go to make it up. Good activity is desirable for its own sake and has pleasure as a concomitant, not as an independent end.

There is considerable merit in explaining many important types of pleasure in terms of activity rather than in terms of a certain sensation. There is pleasure *in* understanding, not just as something resulting from it. There is pleasure *in* aesthetic experience, which involves the employment of abilities for recognition, discrimination, and judgment. There is pleasure *in* succeeding to teach a child how to ride a bicycle or tie shoes. Things that are worth doing can be pleasurable in the doing of them, not because of a particular psychological state resulting from the activity but on account of rational appreciation of them. It is also pleasurable to recall such things, and this is a somewhat different case, but it, too, involves appreciating the worth of what was done or experienced. Many types of pleasure, and particularly enduring ones, depend upon an intentional engagement in certain activities and a judgment of the worth of those activities, even if the activity is a matter of seeking to have certain experiences (such as being present at important points in one's grandchildren's lives).

In discussing pleasure, there is a danger of being reductive and ignoring its many species, causes, and characteristics. The pleasure involved in preparing a fine meal is different from the pleasure of eating when hungry. The pleasure of anticipation is different from the pleasure of experiencing or achieving. The pleasure of smoking is different from the pleasure of having quit smoking. Many of these and others involve certain sensations and also other dimensions having to do with judgments of worth. And there are pain correlates to these. There can be pain in anticipating or imagining something, pain in a failed attempt, and so forth. Frustration, confrontation with unexpected difficulty, confusion, and so forth, are all painful in their way, and the pain, like the pleasures mentioned above, is in part explained by judgments of worth and the character and success of activities.

As Aristotle says: "For pleasure is a state of *soul*, and to each man that which he is said to be a lover of is pleasant; e.g., not only is a horse pleasant to the lover of horses, and a spectacle to the lover of sights, but also in the same way just acts are pleasant to the lover of justice and in general virtuous acts to the lover of virtue" (*N.E.* 1099a 7–11). If one loves aircraft, then watching them, identifying them, learning about them, and talking about them is pleasurable. When it comes to loves and pleasures relevant to character, it matters how they figure in a conception of what is good for human beings. If a person does not enjoy acting justly, he does not have the virtue justice. Acting knowingly, doing the act for the sake of its being that kind of act, doing it from a fixed character, and finding it pleasurable are conditions for the act and the agent being virtuous.

Pleasures that are naturally pleasing cannot simply be listed. Even such pleasures as eating, rest, and sex, which might seem to be paradigmatically naturally pleasing, often need to be regarded in a larger context of understanding and qualification. Resting when one knows one should be working may be pleasurable in the physical sense, but otherwise not. Sexual excitement and climax may be physically pleasurable, but if on account of its occasion or manner it is thought to be wrong, then it is naturally pleasing but only in one sense and not in another. The notion of the naturally pleasant employed here is based upon considerations about what reason rightly endorses. Certain things, such as excellences of character and acting well, are naturally pleasing because of how the causality that produces them is appreciated. A useful notion of the naturally pleasant can be retained if we take it to mean what is desirable for a being with a certain nature. And the determination of what is desirable for a being with a certain nature depends upon an endorsement of reason, an evaluative judgment, not just feeling. That is, we recognize that some activities are such that finding them pleasant, finding in them a reason to commend and pursue them, is concomitant to them. What makes them naturally pleasing is the rationally directed exercise of capacities that structures them.

The involvement of knowledge and activity in what is naturally pleasing is very important. I wish to stress here that there are real goods for humans and that acting in a manner guided by an understanding of them is naturally pleasing, "naturally" in the sense that it is a realization of a good that is a good because of our constitution as rational creatures. There can be activities pleasing to us as *rational* animals on account of our nature, just as there are things pleasing to us on account of our animal nature.

Since pleasures differ according to their activities and their objects, and differ also in their being good or bad, they are not comparable on a single uniform standard. Virtuous and vicious persons do not simply enjoy more or less of the same things. What appears good to them and what they take pleasure in differ in accordance with their characters and in accordance with their practical understanding of the world, so there is not much chance of convincing a bad person to be good by appealing to the prospect of increased pleasure. Bad persons won't see that there is any pleasure or more pleasure in being fairer, more generous, more courageous, more temperate, or whatever. If their understanding of what is worth doing is defective, it is that which needs to be improved. As Annas points out:

> The performance of virtuous deeds, especially those demanded by a virtue like courage, cannot be assessed for pleasure in a way that has appeal to virtuous, vicious, and indifferent alike. The pleasantness of some virtuous actions cannot be appreciated in a way that makes no reference to the viewpoint of the agent, or to his conception of the good life and what it demands of him, or to what is seen by him as valuable.[2]

Our tendencies to choose and act are, in large part, formed by habituated patterns of enjoyment and distaste, and these influence our more mature conceptions of what we think good. If we are firm in bad habits of finding pleasure in what is base or ignoble, it is difficult for us to be motivated to alter these conceptions. This is why early, sustained habituation in desiring what really is good, and in the right way, is crucial not only to having settled dispositions to choose and act well but also to developing an understanding of what makes these good habits. A person is less rationally educable if he is already established in bad habits. He will not be disposed to deliberate well, not having a habituated grasp of the right premises of the reasoning that issues in and justifies good action.

An additional dimension of this view—that the activity of well-ordered practical reason is naturally pleasing—can be identified by considering the ways in which weakness or vice can be painful. The judgment that one has been weak or that one acts from a bad characteristic can be painful and subversive of self-love. There may be pleasure in the act, but recognition of the character of the act (or even the character of the pleasure) may be disturbing and painful. Sometimes we regret having found something pleasurable. We may become angry at ourselves for enjoying hurting another's feelings, for example. Similarly we may become angry at ourselves for failing to stick to a resolution we've made, or for acting unjustly or cowardly. Discovering we have a characteristic we judge to be bad or undesirable is painful. Discovering that we are conflicted because of a desire to do some base thing and the belief that we shouldn't is painful. It may be pleasurable to indulge our appetites but very unpleasant to acknowledge ourselves as intemperate. In fact, looking back on things we have enjoyed, we might not only find it somewhat painful to recall that we enjoyed *that* for those reasons, we might even find it somewhat difficult to believe that we enjoyed it so well at the time. Our understanding of what is worth doing and why is so changed that it may be remarkable to us that we actually had those ends and values or that we rationalized our action in the way we did. For example, we might have felt good about escaping from a threat but now recognize our act as cowardly. And if we recognize an action as, say, cowardly in the very performance of it, that too is painful. The pain need not be a later feeling of remorse or shame. Being intemperate or being cowardly or being dishonest can be painful in itself. Self-possession and self-control do not involve the agitation and conflict that weakness and vice often involve. Not all weakness and vice involve pain, agitation, or conflict. Even a very bad person can exhibit resolve and aplomb. But while genuine possession of a virtue is pleasing and activity arising from it supplies one with a reason to continue to act so, recognition of a weakness or vice can be painful. And failure or refusal to recognize it, while not painful, involves error or self-deception.

The person of poor character needn't be miserable on that account. On the other hand, it is part of Aristotle's view that happiness requires good practical reasoning. The difficulty is not that there is any inconsistency in maintaining both. It is clear that for Aristotle a pleasurable life is not the same thing as a happy life. The difficulty that I wish to focus on concerns how narrowly to construe the sorts of life that can be happy. If a person does not regret the way she has led her life, if she thinks it worthwhile, why not allow that this is enough, as a "good of the soul," to figure in happiness? Aristotle's answer is that there are real norms for happiness, grounded in our nature, and they determine what a genuine good of the soul is. Thinking of one's life as worthwhile is not enough. It must really be worthwhile, and there are real tests for that.

In one sense this is too narrow a view. But it is the right sort of view, and it can be usefully broadened. The idea that there are exercises of our causality that are naturally pleasing in the sense earlier identified is a sound one. But again, we can have norms for this without determining a unique specification. The mob boss running a racket that murders, sells drugs, and extorts protection money can enjoy it and consider himself flourishing. He may even be a hero of sorts to many, uphold the family's honor and tradition, and preside over a corrupt minikingdom with a sense of dignity befitting his high station. Still, "flourishing" of that type *requires* bad character; it is nourished and sustained by vice. It requires commitment to ends that are not endorsed by practical understanding. Being such a person can be naturally pleasing in a perverse sense. That is, one's ego, drive for domination, and sense of being above or outside the law are aggrandized. Only a really bad person could enjoy such a life. This assessment hardly seems arbitrary or a matter of "sour grapes." We can envy someone's wealth, power, and success without admiring them, without wishing to be like *that*, without wishing even to have all that. We may even wonder how they can live with themselves.

What we regard as excellences of character and of practical reason and what we regard as contributing to a happy life need to be generalizable, in the sense that we would regard them similarly in anyone. The mob boss couldn't rationally want to be one among equals in a world of similar characters. What he takes to be good is good for himself, or for himself and his associates, in a way that he could not tolerate in others possessing the same goods. What we can reasonably endorse as counting for success at being a human being, at doing well in exercising one's causality in action and character, cannot be restricted to whom we find it in. What we take to be excellences need to be *human* excellences, not just characteristics that "work" for me or give me or people I care about advantages we enjoy. It is possible to enjoy being bad when one doesn't recognize the badness and sometimes even when one does. Anger, rebellion, and ego can motivate someone to thrive at vice. But that cannot be a conception of successfully leading a human life, and when we speak of someone having sold or lost their soul, in part what we are getting at is that they abdicated or misused practical reason in such a way that they have a corrupt conception of what is good for them. If someone thinks, "Sure, everyone ought to lie, cheat, exploit, and abuse others when it gains an advantage for them," he would be so far gone in corruption of character that there might be no reasoning with him. His conception of good would be out of control and impossible to rationally endorse. He may like being what he has become, but being like that is not something we can accept as a model of a good life or as a life that is naturally pleasing.

A practical and not merely theoretical grasp of human good is needed for an action-guiding grasp of one's own good. When one has this action-guiding grasp (and this is not a grasp of one fixed thing), one's activities are naturally pleasing. What are excellences of character is not a subjective affair, but having them yields a distinctively rich kind of pleasure. It is natural pleasure in the sense that it is caused by the operation of our rational constitution engaged (by habit and reflection) to ends that are really good for it. Living well requires developing a character that one naturally loves having, and to do good for others is to act towards them in a way that serves their real needs and interests and to find it worthwhile and pleasing to do so.

LOVING OUR OWN GOOD

With this background, we can now focus directly on self-love. Self-love is one of the most important goods in a person's life, and it affords rich and stable pleasure. Certainly lack or loss of it is painful. Its ethical dimensions need to be explained further. The main claim is that proper self-love is a concomitant of ethically good activity and that it is not selfish or self-centered.

In the *Nicomachean Ethics* Aristotle writes:

> For men say that one ought to love best one's best friend, and a man's best friend is one who wishes well to the object of his wish for his sake, even if no one is to know it; and these attributes are found most of all in a man's attitude towards himself, and so are all the other attributes by which a friend is defined, for as we have said, it is from this relation that all the characteristics of friendship have extended to our neighbors. (*N.E.* 1168b 1–7)

The good man, he says, should be a lover of self, for the good man obeys his reason and, in so doing, chooses what is best. A good man's action is guided by understanding, and in being a locus of good activity, he is worthy of self-love. Moreover, this self-love is not a matter of examining oneself and consequently regarding oneself with esteem. Rather, a virtuous life is pleasant in itself, a constitutive cause of well-being and not just something one happens to regard with favor or approval. Pleasure is a natural concomitant of the well-functioning of a capacity, and in a life controlled by good practical reasoning, we find desirable for its own sake and worthwhile the rationally directed manner of exercise of our capacities. What we are able to most deeply and enduringly enjoy is, in this sense, ourselves. Self-love is a concomitant of leading a rationally well ordered life guided by a right understanding of human needs, goods, and interests. A good soul loves being good.

A bad person, too, can think well of himself, but in a sense that we regard with reproach. The self-love of a vicious person involves error, ignorance, or illusion. The point is not to promote self-loathing in them but, instead, to help bring about justified self-love through a recognition of and encouragement in doing what is good.

Aristotle held that a bad man will not love himself "because there is nothing in him to love; so that if to be thus is the height of wretchedness, we should strain every nerve to avoid wickedness and should endeavor to be good; for so and only so can one be either friendly to oneself or a friend to another" (*N.E.* 1166b 26–29).

While there are people whose character is wretched but don't feel wretched because of it, Aristotle's claim here is supportable. The notion of self-love that he is employing primarily concerns what sort of engagement one has with the world, what one values and regards as honorable and worthwhile. If a person's evaluative attachments are basically bad, then what they care about and judge to be worthwhile will not in fact be so and they will be unworthy of self-love, even if through self-deception or enjoyment of their activities they maintain some lesser cousin of it. As Aristotle argued in his account of virtue and character, a person is to some extent responsible for what seems good to him, and I would add that a person is similarly responsible to some extent for his conception of his self-worth. These are matters about which it is plain that we can be mistaken.

Aristotle observed that self-love is often regarded with considerable disapproval when it takes the form of egoism or self-centered self-interest. But self-love and pride are not, as such, defects of character. There are, however, conditions they must meet: "Now the man is thought to be proud who thinks himself worthy of great things, being worthy of them" (*N.E.* 1023b 1–2), and "it is with honor that proud men appear to be concerned; for it is honor that they chiefly claim, but in accordance with their deserts" (*N.E.* 1023b 23–24). A proud man is not arrogant. He is worthy of great things, for "greatness in every virtue would seem to be characteristic of a proud man" (*N.E.* 1023b 30–31).

And "the truly proud man must be good" (*N.E.* 1023b 30). This is not just self-importance or lusting after honor and esteem. It is regard for oneself based upon the fact that one loves what is best and thereby merits it. Aristotle's emphasis on honor has in part to do with his view of the publicity of virtue in a social world that is not very large and in which the actions of individuals are not dwarfed by or assimilated into institutions in the ways they often are in modern life. We seek honor as proof of our goodness, not as a substitute for it. Virtuous individuals seek honor from those with practical wisdom "and on the ground of their virtue" (*N.E.* 1095a 29). Whatever the scale of one's society or the institutions in it, virtue requires integrity of agency; it is concerned with things done and not just with the quality of one's will or intentions. At least in that sense, it involves publicity and making a difference in the social world, whatever dimensions the latter has. It also is connected with Aristotle's theory that there is such a thing as genuine human flourishing and its attendant excellences of character and that to act in a way that realizes these is honorable. For the virtuous person, honor is not the exclusive point of his activity; rather, the end is to act in a way that is worthy of honor. The good individual takes pleasure and pride in the right things, being guided by a correct understanding of human good. Such a person enjoys acting well and living well, and the self-love and honor these merit are parts of that enjoyment.

A person is worthy of honor if he aims at what is noble. A virtuous person does so from choice, for its own sake and from a stable character that finds nobility of action pleasurable. The noble, Aristotle says, "is that which is both desirable for its own sake and also worthy of praise; or that which is both good and pleasant because good" (*Rhetoric* 1366 a 33–35). A person who strives to act nobly is worthy of honor, this being "the token of a man's being famous for doing good" (1361 a 27). When discussing honor in the *Rhetoric*, from which this quotation is taken, Aristotle includes among the constituents of honor "sacrifices, commemoration, in verse or prose; privileges; grants of land; front seats at civic celebrations; state burial; statues; public maintenance;" (*Rhetoric* 1361 a 35–38). His treatment of honor in the *Ethics* does not include these sorts of considerations, the focus there being on nobility of action and choosing it for its own sake. Part of the difference in emphasis is surely to be explained by the different purposes of the texts. Looked at from the ethical point of view, including the theory of mind, character, and action that it is connected with, the fundamental consideration about acting honorably is its intrinsic excellence and not the manner in which it is appropriately celebrated or rewarded, the latter being consequent upon the former.

Again, differences in social worlds demand more elasticity in the account of self-love than Aristotle builds into it. For him, self-love is not just a definite good but has a quite definite form, realized in a quite definite type of social world. Relaxing the connection of these social factors to a human function does not relativize the ethical considerations or the normative dimensions of self-love. It does allow for varieties of conditions for its achievement. Some of this has to do with the greater breadth in our conception of human nature, some with the variety of opportunities different social worlds make available. In effect, what we find is not that Aristotle was wrong in some fundamental way but that conditions for achieving self-love are more disjunctively complex than he envisioned. The scope for the good exercise of practical reason can be extended along with our widened range of social forms in which a person can act and live well.

Moreover, there are other senses in which a person can be proud, besides this particular notion of meriting honor. A person can be proud in the sense of an unwillingness to accept assistance or to admit defeat or error. A person can be proud in the sense of prideful or arrogant. And we take pride *in* things: our child's progress, a friend's courage in dealing with adversity, or a national institution or tradition. There is pride in membership, in participation, in ownership, and so on. In each case it makes sense to ask if the pride is merited, if the thing done or identified with really is a credit to us. That is, it makes sense to ask if the pride is grounded in good and what is our part in it or relation to it. This is a respect in which character and one's self-conception primarily concern how one is engaged to the world and what one's own causality brings about. Pride isn't one thing, and there isn't one particular thing to take pride in. Still, pride, as an element of proper self-love, depends upon characteristics and activity. Just being proud ("flag-waving proud" of one's country or organizational affiliations) can be a passion unwarranted by what are taken to be its grounds. It is not to be sneered at, and feelings of solidarity and the upholding of tradition can have considerable merit. But as part of ethically informed self-love, pride is appropriate according to its grounding in how one lives, not just who one is.

Justified pride is pride based upon an understanding of one's merit, and this is quite a different matter from pride based upon the promptings of ego. The former involves self-knowledge, the latter does not. This does not mean that the former is selfless. One should be proud and love oneself for one's excellences and think oneself worthy of good things. But being worthy of them is not automatic, and one's self-love can be more like an egoistic passion than a knowledge of one's merit.

One fairly typical manifestation of self-love is people's unwillingness to admit blame or to accept responsibility. Human beings are remarkably adept at rationalizing error, failure, and incompetence and at distancing themselves from the consequences of their own acts and omissions. They do not want to be accountable for what is shameful or blameworthy and often find it difficult to believe that they could, as agents, really be responsible for some wrong or mistake. Even when people "know better," know full well that what they intend is dishonest, needlessly harmful to others, or unfair, they can manage to convince themselves that it is not wrong or bad if it is done by *them*. Being held responsible can cause remorse or shame, whether it is a matter of being held responsible by others or by one's self. One can (to some extent, anyway) control one's own judgment of oneself and go in for self-deception or grant oneself exemption to the usual strictures.

This is not egoism in the sense of maximizing one's self-interest, but it is a matter of the self being defensive and of the individual being self-centered in order to try to avoid the psychological and other sanctions merited by weakness, error, or vice. This kind of self-centeredness is a way of privileging the self and putting its comfort, so to speak, first. The excellent person is concerned with what sort of individual they are and thinks it is of the first importance to be certain ways, but not out of a sense of privilege or self-aggrandizement. Indeed, the concern of the excellent person for one's self is not particularly self-conscious, since such a person's interests lie mainly in things outside himself, in the purposes, ends, and actions he judges to be worthwhile and important.

There is a natural kind of concern for oneself that it would be implausible to wish away or try to eliminate. Also, it is good to look out for oneself, not in a selfish way, but to ensure that one's legitimate purposes are fulfilled and needs met. We can enhance people's self-love and sense of worth without encouraging them in a crude self-centeredness. A lack of self-love can be painful and frustrating, and it can supply motives for bad action. How we regard ourselves is important to how we regard and treat others, and healthy self-love can enable us to better appreciate and have concern for others. Whether we are generous and sympathetic or mean-minded and unfeeling, whether we are expansive and genuine in our concern for others or exclusively occupied with our own welfare are matters that are strongly influenced by our self-regard. If persons' self-regard is low and they feel that they are unworthy of love or respect, this may be exhibited in their actions overall. They may even put themselves into positions in which they are likely to be victimized or humiliated, or at least fail to stand up for themselves or expect little in the way of credit or acknowledgment. On the other hand, a person with arrogant self-regard may be easily spurred to resentment, vengefulness, and a willingness to belittle and discount others. Sometimes one's self-love is reinforced by, or even primarily based upon, feeling oneself superior to others. In the *Lectures on Ethics,* Kant says: "Men love to compare themselves with others, for by that method they can always arrive at a result favourable to themselves.[3] . . . When I compare myself with another who is better than I, there are but two ways by which I can bridge the gap between us. I can either do my best to attain to his perfections, or else I can seek to depreciate his good qualities."[4]

Comparison to others, unwillingness to admit wrongdoing, the need for the praise of others, and so forth, can all be importantly bound up with the type and intensity of one's self-love. An individual whose self-love is based upon virtue and integrity is less susceptible to this because she is less vulnerable or less in need of certain types of self-assertion, or less dependent upon the opinions of others.

Self-love, like virtue, is not perfect, and, like virtue, it can be corrupted. But a person suffering from guilt or shame or remorse can experience and respond to these in different ways. These states may be appropriate when one has acted badly and reflective of the fact that one indeed does have generally sound character and recognizes a wrong or indiscretion for which he or she takes responsibility. In this sense they are not debilitating. On the other hand, they may be symptomatic of a kind of timidity, insecurity, and lack of self-esteem. People can diminish themselves in their own eyes, deny themselves credit, and refuse to believe they are worthy, capable, or lovable. In such cases a person can labor under a burden of guilt or shame without being bad or foolish in ways that would warrant it. This, too, can make a tremendous difference to whether she sees herself as somehow lesser than or appropriately subservient to others, and whether she believes her own good is something that others can and should take seriously. Part of sound self-love is that one is strong enough to be concerned for the good of others and also thinks that one's own good is an appropriate object of others' concern. The self-lover may be too proud to grovel, but not too proud to seek help, advice, and encouragement, not out of weakness but out of a recognition of what is required to live, choose, and act well.

There is an important relation between self-love and prudence. Prudence has been understood in a number of ways: as self-interest, as practical foresight in the way that Nagel explains it in *The Possibility of Altruism*, and as practical wisdom in the more classical sense. These three are not mutually exclusive, or at least not necessarily. Practical foresight and pursuing self-interest can surely be elements of practical wisdom if some interpretive elasticity is permitted. But there are important differences in emphasis. Self-interest is often interpreted in terms of desire-satisfaction, or at least of putting one's own case first. Nagel's account of practical foresight focuses on formal features of reasons and what he takes to be the temporal neutrality of good reasons. He says that "a person's future should be of interest to him not because it is among his present interests, but because it is his *future*."[5] And "practical judgments, like other kinds of judgments, are consonant with the conception of oneself as a temporally extended being for whom the future is no less real than the present. This conception requires that one be able to view all times, including the present, from a standpoint of temporal neutrality."[6]

Practical wisdom's focus is different. It focuses on knowledge of good and its role in shaping deliberation and orienting virtues of character in choice and action. I have already argued that self-love is not egoistic. In fact, proper self-love cannot be achieved egoistically, since it is causally dependent upon pursuit of goods that are not ego-situated. Also, while there are goods for each person as an individual, many of them are not subjectively based or based upon what one's desires happen to be. When one exercises practical reason well, its exercise can in turn be the cause of certain desires, in that the person understands what sorts of things it is worth caring about and pursuing. This kind of self-love is achieved through a causality that, in order to succeed, must be outward-looking, in that it is informed by world-guided understanding. Practical foresight is part of this as well, where foresight includes realizing that what one does makes a difference to who one is and becomes. In this respect, prudence is crucial to self-love, rather than the latter being an egoistic motivational basis of the former.

For the egoist the world is basically a resource, a resource to be exploited for purposes driven by self-interest, and norms of practical reason are norms for the efficient use of this resource. Consequently, for ethical egoism the weight that facts have as considerations for practical reason is in an important way person-relative. It will depend upon subjective considerations about the individual. In this respect, practical reason's authority is derivative or subordinate. The problem with this is that it involves an impoverished conception of both the objects and the prescriptivity of practical reason. It assigns to reason a practical function—ascertaining how to realize one's interests. While one's own desires and interests have an urgency and are objects of immediate concern in a way that those of others may not be, they are not privileged just for that and are not different in kind just for that. A conception of what is worth doing and the reasons for it is a conception that is not ego-situated or essentially relative to the individual who has it. Practical reason's teleology is properly aimed at what it is good to do. This is not conceptually or empirically linked to egoism. Reason's authority is authority for each individual but is not subjective. One's concern for his or her own projects and circumstances is legitimate, and morality does not deny its legitimacy. Self-love, though, is achieved through appreciating the weight of considerations about good action and good characteristics that reason understands to be general and to be based upon facts about the world (including human nature). Prudence, in this wider, richer sense of an action-guiding understanding, is a condition for self-love and for the practical self-knowledge that practical reasoners can enjoy in a distinctive way.

REVISING ARISTOTLE'S VIEW

There are several considerations about subjectivity that are not part of Aristotle's account of self-love but surely are very important. His conception of the rational agent is quite different from most post-Cartesian conceptions of the self, and he shows little interest in introspective or phenomenological concerns that in modern philosophy are often central. The more "vertical" conceptions of mind, motive, and levels of consciousness and attendant issues of self-deception, rationalization, neurosis, and so forth, are not found in his account. Room for them should be made. On the other hand, Aristotle's view is a potent antidote to the ill effects of exaggerated concern with subjectivity and the character and texture of self-consciousness. The self as a rational agent is formed from the outside-in as well as from the inside-out. That is, it is people's understanding of and engagement with the world that in important respects makes them who they are. There are things to know and attend to with respect to questions of value and the objects of practical reason, and these are obscured or ignored by many currents of modern thought, which begin only with the content and perspective of the self as subject.

Aristotle's bias to the world rather than to the subject (who is for him primarily a knower and an agent, not a locus of perspective) is reflected in the way in which his conception of self-love does not involve self-absorption or self-interest. Rational self-love is an achievement, not a starting point. Rational self-interest is a matter of having a sound conception of what is in one's interest, where the notion of the rational concerns content as well as form. This is not a matter that can be exhaustively settled from the inside-out. It requires an understanding of what is in a self's interest or a rational agent's interest, an understanding that itself can be better or worse, improved or degraded, with respect to considerations that not only are not ego-situated or subjective but depend upon what the world is like. In this respect, the notion of self-interest needs to be broadened in order to register these normative considerations. Someone can be self-interested in the familiar, narrow sense, but in addition there are interests of the self that not only need not be selfish but require a practical knowledge of the world.

Joseph Raz has argued that well-being needs to be distinguished from self-interest.

> Well-being is sometimes understood as a rough synonym of self-interest. The use of these notions reflects both moral convictions and beliefs about human motivation. According to some the two notions are indeed broadly interchangeable. While regarding 'interest' as roughly co-extensive with "well-being," I shall follow a slightly different and narrower usage of "self-interest." In a nutshell, self-interest is largely a biological notion. Frustrating any of a person's biologically determined needs and desires is in itself against his self-interest, unless it instrumentally serves to improve the satisfaction of these needs and desires of his in

> the long run, or unless it prolongs his life, or protects him from danger.[7]

To judge a person's well-being, he says, is to judge "the success or failure of his life, not the means for that success or failure."[8] Well-being concerns one's life as a whole and one's goals and the reasons for them. "Self-interest is what remains after subtracting from the wider notion of well-being success in those projects whose value (in the eye of the person in question) is their contribution to the well-being of others."[9]

We do not have to endorse this in its details in order to see the point of distinguishing a narrow version of self-interest from other interests of the self. The latter depend heavily on the manner in which practical reason is employed (not just in fulfilling them but in formulating them), in that they involve conceptions of worth and an understanding of what kind of a world it is and what kind of a life it is possible and good to live.

The self-love of Aristotle's excellent individual is a reflection in that person of his attachment to what is good. While Aristotle's account of self-love and pride can seem lacking in phenomenological dimensions and while it is *harder* to know how to live than his discussion may suggest, much of its merit lies in how it gives a foothold for judgments of worth in a public, objective order. It indicates ways in which the self is informed and oriented and given substance by knowledge of the world. According to Aristotle, a mind is, in a sense, what it thinks, and it does not think without objects. A character is, in a sense, what it cares about and what it does, and these are guided by a conception of objects and their value. Valuation need not be a matter of projection or subjective creation. Indeed, if the arguments of chapter 1 hold up, it cannot be such. Perception, thought, and judgment interpreted realistically are ineliminable parts of sound valuation. There are factual considerations to attend to and things to know concerning what is worth doing. Given our constitution, some things are needed by us, are good for us, serve our interests and well-being. The activity of practical reason and the business of living are, to some extent, searches for understanding of these matters and also exercises of that understanding. The surest self-knowledge and the self-love that can be its concomitant are based upon a knowing engagement with the world and are not self-centered or self-absorbed. In one respect, a narrow concern with self-interest is indicative of ignorance of anything worth pursuing, and of the error of thinking that, simply because I care about it, it is important. Granted there are many drives and impulses to answer to and to acknowledge. And it is not necessary, in order to be a self-lover, to be guided self-consciously by a distinctively ethical conception of one's life. One may strongly identify with various kinds of concerns and ideals. But there are still important, common factors involved in leading a kind of life in which self-love is a realized good. One may take aesthetic creativity, professional success, or dedication to a cause as his guiding, driving concern. Maybe self-love is not even particularly important to him; these or other sorts of things may come first or even displace self-love as a concern. It is surely possible to do admirable, valuable, excellent things even if that is so. In any case, self-love is not achieved by aiming at it. It is achieved by striving to lead a life of projects and concerns that one has rational confidence are worthwhile. But not to achieve self-love is to have a significant lacuna in one's life, and whatever good one does or whatever meaningfulness one confers on his life, without self-love it will be a life that is in an important way frustrated.

It is not implausible to hold that, given human psychology, there are (broad and elastic but real) conditions on leading a life in which and through which one's own activity is enjoyed as valuable. Moreover, what Aristotle recognizes as virtues are not straight lines on a blueprint design for living. They are not strategies to follow to get happy results. They are an outline of the most central characteristics one needs in order to do well in the general business of living. Granted he does detail many virtues and at times makes a number of quite specific observations about what constitutes virtuous acts under specific headings. But while the details give content and vivacity to the particular conception of a good life he endorsed, we can see the virtues in a broader perspective. We need certain characteristics in order to lead not just distinctively ethical lives but to live well generally. Aristotle does argue that there is a best life and that it involves a certain harmony of exercise of capacities, and this may well be too circumscribed a view. Even if it is one of the excellent lives we could live, it is not the one that everyone would rationally choose as best. But the kind of psychology of self-love endorsed here both allows for more possibilities than Aristotle countenanced and retains much of the form of his conception of a good life. We do not have to accept Aristotle's metaphysical teleology or concur with his confidence that an unequivocally best kind of life is ascertainable from an understanding of our nature to take normatively based self-love as a fundamental good achievable only in certain ways.

The following claims summarize the main points of the chapter and serve as a transition to the treatment of friendship.

(1) Self-love in its primary sense means regarding oneself as worthy of good because one is productive of good.
(2) To properly judge oneself as worthy of good requires a degree of practical wisdom.
(3) Self-love includes a rich and stable type of enjoyment, produced by one's activity in accordance with an understanding of human good.

Self-love is ethically significant because of the role of practical comprehension of value in it and because of its role in human well-being. We will find correlates to both of these, and also important causal relations to self-love, in the account of friendship.

CHAPTER 4

Friendship

The importance of friendship in our lives hardly needs to be argued for, although there is much to reflect on and try to be clear about. Discussing it is also a way of bringing ethical discussion closer to issues that all are familiar with and that do not suffer from artificiality. Several aspects of the topic will be taken up here, including the relations between friendship and self-love, the role of friendship in self-knowledge, and the ways in which the practical employment of reason gives friendships their character. Each of these is an ethical dimension of friendship. As in the discussion of self-love, Aristotle will again be extensively relied upon, and again there will be revisions of and departures from his account. But the Aristotelian spirit of the discussion is plain: friendship is a fundamental human good, its nature depending upon our psychology and the exercise of practical reason.

Self-love, we argued, is a crucial part of living well. So too is friendship. We need friends to do good for and to do good for us. Friends, in the primary sense, are partners in virtue. They share each other's company and appreciate and encourage each other's excellences. Friendship is not just one of the happy advantages of having successfully integrated oneself into social life. Rational animals are social beings, only capable of living the life and realizing the goods distinctive of them in society. We learn to act, produce, reason, and inquire in social life.[1] Moreover, it is not just that social life is necessary for the realization of human potentialities; it is something nearly everyone desires for its own sake. The companionship, cooperation, richly textured communication, and vast variety of practices, arts, and undertakings that mark human social life are goods we would not choose to be without. Friendship is a relation between people that sustains and motivates these features of our lives, contributing to the discovery and exploration of all variety of human goods and interests.[2]

Humans are capable of action guided by understanding of goods, and they are also capable of shared understanding of them. Ants, wolves, and bees are social animals, but they are social in having various role-specific instincts and behaviors. They do not share in articulating and acting in accordance with conceptions of good in the way humans do. Our judgments of what is pleasurable and worthwhile are based upon testable, revisable conceptions of the world, including our own nature. Our judging something to be good is an exercise of reason, as is our decision to aim to do it or have it. Our own appetites and motives are objects of rational assessment and revision. We are also capable of forming a conception of another's good and being motivated by it. Friendship, in this sense, is a distinctively human excellence. Humans form and discuss and revise shared conceptions of significance, and it would be impossible to lead human lives without them. We can love animals and especially love our pets, and they can, in their way, show affection, loyalty, and desire for our company. But they cannot love us as we love each other, and we cannot love them in the same way we love human friends. There is not the mutual knowledge of the same goods and the capacity to be motivated by it that characterize human friendship. If a man's best friend or only friend is a dog, he is pretty near friendless. Animals have their own goods, which we often wish to protect and promote. They are not merely instruments for us. They are capable of goods in their lives appropriate to their species-specific natures, and we can enjoy and contribute to them. But their goods are not just the same as ours, and we cannot relate to them nor they to us in some of the ways that make friendship one of the excellences of our lives.

Aristotle's lengthy discussion of friendship in books 8 and 9 of the *Nicomachean Ethics* addresses a large number of different friendship relations, including parent to child, ruler to subject, and others containing inequalities. Still, one is left with the impression that his focal idea of friendship is that of men in their forties. When we see how he characterizes self-love and the relation between self-love and friendship, this impression is easily reinforced. In some ways, though, this is an error of focus, not a fundamental flaw in his understanding of friendship and self-love. He is certainly right that friendship is not just a pleasurable accessory to living well. He is also right to notice that friendship can take a variety of forms depending upon the relations of those involved. Parents are friends to their children in different ways than peers are friends to each other, and friendships between old and young differ in still other ways. What is common to sound friendships is attention to human good. Parents can be friends to their children in part by habituating them well. This is one form that concern for their good takes. If mature people are friends in the primary sense through being partners in virtue, then being a friend to a child involves enabling and encouraging him or her to become the sort of person in whom human excellences are realized. Since children have so little rational, deliberative control over their conceptions of what is good and since the habits formed in them strongly inform their character, loving them requires wisdom in habituating them to be pleased by what is good. In other sorts of relationships this same focal concern with good is the core of friendship.

WHAT ARE FRIENDS FOR?

Friendship, Aristotle says, is to be understood in much the same way as self-love.

> Friendly relations with one's neighbors, and the marks by which friendships are defined, seem to have proceeded from a man's relation to himself. For (1) we define a friend as one who wishes and does what is good, or seems to, for the sake of his friend, or (2) as one who wishes his friend to exist and live, for his sake; which mothers do to their children, and friends do who have come into conflict. And (3) others define him as one who lives with and (4) has the same tastes as another, or (5) one who grieves and rejoices with his friend; and this too is found in mothers most of all. It is by some one of these characteristics that friendship too is defined.
>
> Now each of these is true of the good man's relation to himself. (*N.E.* 1166a 1–10)

In this passage and in several others in book 9, Aristotle does seem to argue that friendship not only has likenesses to self-love but is, as it were, an extension of it. Aristotle argues that in the best friendships friends are alike in reason in that they are similar in good character. That is how a friend is like another self. Reason is the capacity to know what is good for humans in general. It is not just a power to maximize ego-centered goal achievement or one's own good.[3] There are *human* goods, and a self-lover and a good friend aim at those. Nobility is a greater good than wealth or success, but it is so because it is consequent upon what reason tells us is best, and it is not just a matter of aggrandizement of the self. Moreover, Aristotle is quite clear that friends delight in the perception of each other and in each other's existence, and in sharing their lives. A friend's goodness is like one's own, but not lovable merely because of the likeness to oneself. In both one's own case and that of the other, it is the goodness of this, that, and the other particular thing about the individual which is lovable. This point is perhaps best made by considering what is lost in the loss of a friend. It is, in a sense, a loss of part of one's life, but a part that was unique, external, and significant because of its own independent existence. A friend is like another self in some ways, but what is delightful about a friend is not just the likeness to oneself but the existence of the other as *that* individual. This is a point that deserves more emphasis than Aristotle gives it, especially when we see (a bit later) how enjoyable it can be to have friends who are unlike oneself in various ways.

What is it about someone's being *that* individual that we love? Their uniqueness is perhaps a matter of causal origin, but it is not the metaphysics of modality that engages our interest and affection. When we love someone for himself or herself, it is the actualization of human good in the person and our intimate acquaintance with it that we love. Someone's qualities are the basis for being thought well of, but it is on account of our knowledge of a person that he or she is lovable as a friend and not just worthy of esteem or respect. Reason tells us what is lovable, and experience, in particular the experience of sharing conceptions of good and sharing activities that realize it or bring it about, makes us friends.

When Aristotle says that a friend is another self and that what is distinctive of friendship is most fully realized in a virtuous person's self-regard, he is not making friendship derivative of or a shadow of self-love. Rather, he is pointing to the fact that in proper self-love, a person identifies with and gratifies what is best in herself, seeking what is genuinely good because it is good, and that such a self-lover loves her friend in a similar way. He nowhere argues that friends are properly instruments of self-aggrandizement or self-interest. We *need* friends, not as instruments but because being able to exercise the virtues and enjoying their exercise in others are parts of a good life.

Friendship is not an overflow from self-sufficiency but a part of it, a part in and through which one learns what is good, how to judge and how to act. This is also why he discusses so many different friendship relations, those between citizens, between parents and children, ruler and ruled, master and slave, and others. In each of them the activity of friendship is to conduce to the good of those in the relationship. He is certainly right that we need friends. Even those who are excellent in character and beneficiaries of good fortune need them. Knowing and loving our friends is part of our own good.

It is relevant here to ask how it is that people come to have conceptions of their self-interest or their own good. I have argued that human goods, needs, and interests are, in an important respect, cognitive matters; there are things to *know* about human nature and the world with respect to these. We learn our interests and develop our conceptions of worth in action and experience. We find out what we're capable of, what pleases us, what engages us, what is worth sacrifice or risk, in our activities and relations with others. We find out what our emotions and inclinations are and what we have tolerance for and patience with, and so forth, in social life. The content and ordering of our aims, priorities, and commitments and also a good deal of the development of our emotions, imagination, and sensibility are crucially shaped by our involvements with others. What is meant by being responsible for our actions and our character is learned in experience with others. No one could figure out alone how to live and what is his good, nor could he develop capacities for self-determination alone.

Even Aristotle, for whom there was a conception of the well-functioning of human nature, did not have a theory (in any formal sense) of how to realize it or what to do in all cases. We have to judge in each case, and judgment is not mechanical rule following. As Sarah Broadie in *Ethics with Aristotle* notes, commenting on Aristotle's view: "Not even the wisest moralist can firmly lay down general rules for good or right action, since only the agent in each case can know then and there what is best. There is no recipe for 'functioning well.' "[4] We find out how to judge, how to reason about value, what to expect of and reasonably require of ourselves and others as we go along. For example, one can learn a great deal about what counts as healthy emotionality in friendship. We become angry with our friends just as we become angry with others, but it can be important to us not to ruin a friendship because of our anger. So we realize that perhaps we haven't been altogether fair, or that we're being selfish, or that even if our anger is fully justified, it is not worth spoiling the friendship over the cause of it. People who really do work at being friends work at being less selfish, less manipulative, more fair-minded. They recognize that relations between people needn't be adversarial or suspicious or self-serving and that it can be pleasurable in a distinctive way to be actively concerned for the good of another. Friendship is a context in which one can learn how another's needs can take priority over one's own feelings or desires. It is not just that one is likely to be more decent to one's friends, more considerate of their needs and feelings. Rather, it is in friendships that one is apt to acquire those traits in the first place. We generally do not have a fully formed character to bring to friendships. We develop much of our character in our friendships, for better or worse. Friendship is not simply a context for the employment of practical reason. We learn what to do, how to respond, what is helpful, what is poisonous between people to a large extent in the details of living with and caring about others. Whether we have practical wisdom or not is in large part a matter of what sorts of friendships we have. While one cares more for one's friends than for others and is more concerned to be good to them, part of what is so important about friendship is that it is there that we find out most concretely and immediately what people are like and how to act along with them and what to do for them.

The business of living is not practice at realizing goods known in advance. It is *learning* what is good, what our needs are, what is delightful, what is awful, and what is indifferent. If we no longer endorse the idea that there is a single condition of harmonious, well-functioning of human capacities, then the question of what is good and how to realize it is, in a sense, even more difficult. What structure knowledge of human good has is the result of reflection upon and organization of the contents and form of practical reason in operation. We learn in experience what to aim at, what to attend to, how to weigh it and coordinate it with other considerations. And a great deal of this experience gets its contours from friendships. We are more willing to listen to our friends, be persuaded by them, have confidence in their opinions. And people about whom we feel these things are more likely to become our friends. Friendships are a crucial source for our knowledge of human nature and human good.

Moreover, while friends can be rivals in various ways, they do not resent each other's successes or feel diminished by each other's gain in honor. The objects of good people's judgments of worth are typically not susceptible to an economic analysis wherein the agents are egos battling for "market share" or competitive advantage. Honor, happiness, success, admiration, and so forth, surely are goods that in many contexts cannot be distributed equally. But to a virtuous person what is good is not consequent upon the fact that it satisfies *my* desire or that *I've* got more of it than you.

The good individual wishes for what is good and "to live and be preserved," and this is also what we wish for our friends. In sound friendships each recognizes the other as a locus of good activity and as deserving what is good because of this. I shall argue below that friendship is not just an additional good to the self-lover but is a condition for self-love.

Friendship is more than good will and mutual affection. It is an activity structured by practical reason, a right understanding of goods. This will not be exactly similar across persons, but there will be a shared grasp of the general contours of human interest and need. Someone is lovable because they are a locus of good activity, and in being such, they will want and promote our good in the activity of friendship. Friends, in the primary sense, want each other to be virtuous and recognize and enjoy each other's excellences.

Moreover, much of our knowledge of our own character depends upon friendship. In having friends who are good and who we know to be good, we are able to recognize and confirm our own goodness. Virtuous friends are not only examples of goodness but, as such, are standards by which to know ourselves. This is one crucial way in which a friend is like another self. In our recognition of another's virtue, we are enabled to discern and assess our own. A good friend is an example of *human* excellence, not just someone we have affection for or feel attraction to. As such, a virtuous friend realizes excellences we rightly value, and even if we do not strive to be just like them, our knowledge of them increases our knowledge of our own abilities, commitments, and excellences.

Friendship is one of the primary settings in which practical reason is educated. It is in friendships that we are often best able to learn how to deal with our own and others' emotions, how to resolve conflicts, how to forgive, overcome resentment, and make the well-being of others a central issue of our own concern. We learn so much about ourselves in friendships because of the emotionality they involve, the tests of good faith and loyalty they impose, and the demands on our willingness to understand another's perspective, circumstances, and self-conception. In friendships we employ our practical reason on behalf of another, and sometimes have to employ it in ways that our own individual circumstances would not otherwise motivate.

Moreover, with very few exceptions the purposes and projects in which human capacities are pleasurably exercised are either to some extent cooperative or at least are supported and made more enjoyable by sharing. Unless you have a highly eccentric conception of what is enjoyable and worthwhile in what you undertake, you want to see yourself as participating in an activity that, while a good to you, is not a good only on account of the fact that it is you engaging in it. The self is the locus of interest and valuing, but this person-relativity is not the sole basis of what is interesting and worthwhile. Stamp collecting, pastry baking, appreciating music, hiking, getting a handle on quantum physics, and just about anything else humans enjoy and see a worthwhile point in not only can be engaged in cooperatively but are made more interesting and more enjoyable and are better done and appreciated when integrated into or at least connected to the activities of others. This is also an ongoing potential basis for friendships.[5] In joint activity we often come to enjoy and value more fully the activity and also those with whom we participate in it. Friendship is a way of coming to value both undertakings and those engaged in them.

In wanting and striving for the good of a friend, we are not merely giving of our own good, we are enlarging it by incorporating something else into it that augments it. A friend is a distinct individual with his or her own interests and good, but friendship based on a true conception of good does not see this as fragmentation or as interference with oneself. Rather, there is shared rational appreciation of human good and shared activity that realizes it. It is delightful to be alike in judgment and deliberation and to share not only conceptions of goods but pursuit of them. Good friends enable us to know ourselves better both by participating closely in our lives and by being distinct. As Cooper put it, "The presumption is that even an intimate friend remains distinct enough to be studied objectively; yet because one intuitively knows oneself to be fundamentally the same in character as he is, one obtains through him an objective view of oneself."[6] It is the likeness in reason that enlarges and informs our conception of ourselves. A friend is to some extent a reflection of myself and enables me to see my own character more clearly, at least when the friendship involves thoughtfulness and real mutual concern.

THE SOCIAL CONTEXT OF FRIENDSHIP

How people see themselves and others depends in part upon social factors. If one lives and works in a setting dominated by egoistic competition, then rivalry, emulation, and acquisition will likely be very important. It may be important to endorse publicly values of fair play and reward in proportion to effort and the importance of individuals and their rights, although it is masking dishonesty, greed, and the willingness or even the desire to ruin or at least "defeat" others. Writing about business and economic life in 1923, Frank Knight, in "The Ethics of Competition," noted:

> It seems evident that most of the ends which are actually striven after in the daily lives of modern peoples are primarily of this character; they are like the cards and checker-men, worthless (at best) in themselves, but the objects of the game; and to raise questions about the game is to make one's self disagreeable. To "play the game" is the current version of accepting the universe, and protest is blasphemy; the Good Man has given place to the "good sport." In America particularly, where competitive business, and its concomitant, the sporting view of life, have reached their fullest development, there have come to be two sorts of virtue. The greater virtue is to win; and meticulous questions about the methods are not in the best form, provided the methods bring victory. The lesser virtue is to go out and die gracefully after having lost.[7]

Knight was a conservative economist and not a critic of capitalist economics. He was, nevertheless, a severe critic of how economic thinking and valuation tended to displace ethical thinking and valuation, and he was an astute observer of how the assumptions of economic theory diverge from reality in ways that are socially and ethically very disturbing. One of his points that is particularly relevant to the present discussion is that a set of economic arrangements that encourages rivalry, emulation, and acquisition in an ever-accelerating way requires everyone to accept the values of the system or suffer severely for it:

> In a social order where all values are reduced to the money measure in the degree that this is true of modern industrial nations, a considerable fraction of the most noble and sensitive characters will lead unhappy and even futile lives. Everyone is compelled to play the economic game and be judged by his success in playing it, whatever his field of activity or type of

> interest, and has to squeeze in as a sideline any other competition or non-competitive activity, which may have for him greater intrinsic appeal.[8]

There are plenty of people who enthusiastically play the "game" and who enjoy thinking of themselves as aggressively self-seeking and self-promoting. And this, of course, is not likely to be confined to work or working hours. They develop a motivational structure, a set of attitudes and an outlook on life in general. Even people who aren't enthusiastic about the "game" or who positively reject or abhor it are required to play, at least enough not to lose completely. The social setting will be pervaded by the egoism, acquisitiveness, and contempt for virtue that are marks of so many of the leading players and would-be leaders. It can become part of the social atmosphere at all socioeconomic levels and in all spheres of life. In such a situation there may be dramatically diminished valuing of and effort toward cooperation, mutual concern, regard, sympathy for the welfare of others, and even friendship. Of course, not everyone becomes aggressively self-seeking and estranged from or suspicious of others, and competition can also encourage integrity, mutual respect, and concern for more than one's own good. But large-scale social and economic arrangements and conditions and the kinds of rationales that are given for them can have a considerable effect on what sorts of personal relationships people have because of prevalent attitudes about what counts as successful or admirable or in people's interests, and what counts as good practical reasoning.

It would be a mistake to try to fashion more than a very few generalizations about this. Competition can encourage self-esteem and mutual appreciation. Prosperity makes some people generous and interested in the plight of others, and it makes some people self-important and self-concerned. One way in which aggressively egoistic competition is undermining of friendship is that it places low value on the idea of people deliberately pursuing common goods or of there even being common goods. When this is combined with the thought that practical reasoning is confined to maximizing preference-satisfaction and that there is no rational assessment of preferences, the effect is even more powerful. This is, in large part, what troubled Knight, i.e., the displacement of rational thinking about value by purely economic thought. The assumptions of economic theory are powerful, appropriate tools for a variety of purposes. But when its idealizations and simplifications are widely taken up as general action-guiding principles, this often drives out substantive rational thought about value. People have always taken advantage of each other and abused others or been cynical or apathetic, and these vices are not confined to one or another type of social world. Still, social conventions and cultural norms influence the character of practical reasoning. They provide criteria of what counts as success, and they shape people's expectations of each other.

FRIENDSHIP AND ETHICAL LEARNING

The friendships we form and want and try to have both reflect and inform character. They are a crucial means of ethical maturation. It is in the detailed life of a friendship that people learn generosity, willingness to help, and patience, and learn also that there are things about other human beings that we simply cannot tailor to our own ideals, preferences, or needs. It is also in friendship that we learn that while each person's happiness is a good to him, it is both possible and pleasing to be concerned with it and to contribute to the good of another for his own sake. Because genuine friendship involves a concern to understand a person, the attention paid to him is part of our education of sensibility and is instructive about human nature. Our friends are people we know in some detail, and that knowledge can contribute to our being more skilled and accurate in ethically relevant description. Our knowledge of friends cannot be simply generalized over people, but it is a resource for reasoning about human good.

Friendships do sometimes sour or just fade, or a particular episode can undo them. It is not only in the successes that we learn about ourselves and human nature more generally. Friendship is work, and one's vulnerabilities, sensibility, and convictions can be powerfully tested in it as people sort out the details of what they want to know and show. Moreover, it is often people who know you best who are able to be cruelest or most abusive. They know your weaknesses and the bases of your self-esteem. Being ill-served by someone you thought was a friend is especially disappointing and painful. There is always more to know about people, and we sometimes find it out in the worst ways. Sound friendships survive a variety of vicissitudes—rivalry, separation, periods of self-absorption, and so on. While there is no guarantee against their being damaged or undone, they are not constantly shadowed by fear of this but, rather, sustained by their potential for continuing enjoyment and increase in mutual knowledge. A friend's interests and activities and even emotions represent possibilities for us, ways of regarding the world and ourselves. Friendships can broaden the range of things we appreciate, regard as important, and find humor in. In this respect, friendship is, especially at the beginning, experimental. It tests our range of concern and attention and motivates us to undertake things we might not consider on our own. It is, in a sense, an experimental way of finding out what is good. When friendships go wrong, reflection upon how and why can illuminate aspects of motivation we were ignorant of or naive about and can prompt us to reconsider how well our conceptions of others is really congruent with what they are like and to what extent they are biased by our own needs and desires. Consider also how bad it is not to have friends. Its badness is not just loneliness but a lack of confirmation and caring acknowledgment by others, as well as a way of being cut off from goods achievable by cooperation. This can lead to self-absorption and a narrowing of one's appreciation of others. Lack of friends is not only unpleasant; it can be damaging. It can be alienating and lead to a kind of emotional selfishness and an unwillingness to be involved with others and open with them. These sorts of effects on a person's character can further distance him from others and leave him to think more and more about himself, something which tends to result in unhappiness and misperceptions of the motives, needs, and feelings of others.

We wish to find more to appreciate in our friends, and we want to be better able to do good for them. If, for example, they feel resentment or suspicion, we want to know why and enable them to overcome it, for their own sake. We don't want our friends to be overcome with hate or fear, or for their rationality and well-being to be compromised. One reason knowledge of the individual is important is that we want our friends to love themselves, and we need to have considerable knowledge of them to contribute to that end. Good friends encourage each other's understanding of his or her own motives. A good friend is not only someone who is better able than others to judge when you are betraying your own convictions or trying to disown your own desires or emotions; he or she is also someone for whom you *want* to keep your own integrity intact.

FRIENDSHIP AND KNOWLEDGE

Both friendship and self-love require knowledge of general matters and knowledge of the individual. Self-love requires an understanding of what is good for beings constituted as we are, and it also requires self-knowledge, an understanding of one's own character, which is in part an understanding of the bases of one's judgments of worth. This is important in friendship as well. To be a friend to someone, we need to have knowledge of her as an individual. We need to have a sense of what concerns and moves the person and how she regards things and what are her complexities of character. General knowledge of human good, self-knowledge, and knowledge of the other are complexly interrelated, no one of them prior to the others. These are all dimensions of practical knowledge.

There is a debate in the literature on Aristotle over whether in friendships based upon utility or pleasure, there is goodwill for the sake of the other or one does well for the other only out of self-interest.[9] Our project here is not textual analysis or construction of a taxonomy of friendships. In any case, it is true that friendships can be mixed in motive and that in those that are less than fully sound and enduring, concern for each other's good and appreciation of it is not altogether stable. Aristotle's notion of perfect friendship is so closely linked to his conception of a specific way of being an excellent person that it can be quite determinately characterized. There is a definite notion of human excellence, and excellent people are fixed and unchangeable in character. Both of these claims are idealizations, and there surely are good people and good friendships that do not fully instantiate them. But the important truth in his view is that the interpretation of friendship is centered around human good and practical reason.

In lesser friendships, the good that each is mainly concerned with is one's own and not the good that can be achieved by or for the other person as well as oneself. Because of this, knowledge of the other need not be as complete, and the other's friendship is in some ways more easily substitutable, or at least his own good is not a primary concern to the person whose friend he is. The mutual participation in each other's life is less, and such friends do not see each other as fully sharing in activity. In these lesser friendships, we do not see the other as "another self." As A. W. Price puts it: "One and the same act may count as contributing, as a constituent and not a cause, to the *eudaimonia* of two persons. It is this possibility that grounds Aristotle's ideal of friendship."[10] Aristotle's account requires virtuous friends to be alike in virtue and to perceive and judge in the same way. While friends are alike in being virtuous in the best friendships, it would be implausibly restrictive to require them to have just the same virtues to the same degree. After all, sometimes it is differences in character and judgment that we appreciate in others. Their goodness need not be altogether uniform with our own. For a number of good reasons, we are more willing to accommodate a wider range of personal ideals and excellences than Aristotle allowed. Integrity and soundness of character may have certain highly general properties, and there are many matters upon which virtue speaks in a single voice. But Aristotle's discussion leaves too little room for differences of character and individual purposes and ideals. I argued earlier that there being real human goods does not require that there be an intrinsic end for human nature, the specification of which will determine those goods. It would be a mistake to ascribe complete fixity and definition even to Aristotle's account, since there is for him no formula for excellence. Nonetheless, happiness is for him an intrinsic end, the virtues are constitutive means to it, and there is at least a characterization of the great-souled man, the excellent specimen of human nature. But there are more ways of succeeding at realizing excellences of human nature than Aristotle's great-souled man, and it would be a mistake to take friendships between such individuals as uniquely paradigmatic. Moreover, while excellent people may appreciate each other's virtues, they may not feel much affection for or interest in each other. Their concerns and perspectives may be different enough, their temperaments sufficiently incompatible that they just don't care much for each other. There are too many possible developments of human character and ability for us to plausibly suppose that even if there is a best kind of friendship, there is a quite specific type of person in it.

Moreover, one of the marks of lasting, sound friendship is toleration of each other's minor vices. We may even find it endearing that our friend has a slightly annoying habit or a particular mannerism or fault. We don't expect our friends to be perfect, and we can particularly appreciate their willingness to admit weaknesses or blemishes of character when this is not indicative of self-contempt. It is more important to us that they know themselves than that they have no faults. Friends are tolerant of these but do not indulge them to the point of encouraging them. Nor do they play the role of virtue police or interfere with each other's autonomy and privacy of thought and feeling.[11] Indeed, one aspect of good friendship is respecting the privacy of thought and feeling, even where we think we know each other through and through. We are not as transparent to ourselves or to others as many of us would like to believe, and even when we know someone well, we never know anyone completely. But people who are good friends to each other have good judgment about leaving something of each other to themselves.

There is an additional respect in which Aristotle's account somewhat oversimplifies the actual situation. Virtue and friendship can conflict in ways he did not really consider. Our loyalty to a friend may be what motivates us to act unjustly toward someone else. On the other hand, our commitment to fairness may in some circumstances seem to a friend to amount to a betrayal of him. This sort of tension is not a difficulty peculiar to the context of friendship; it may be an instance of the general problem of the relations of the virtues. But it does seem that our earlier remark that friends are partners in virtue needs to be qualified. Virtue and friendship can pull in different directions. Nor is it going to be much help to suggest that considerations of justice, for example, are overriding, that they take priority over considerations of friendship. Part of the difficulty is knowing what justice requires. It may be wrong to lie or cheat for a friend or to see that he is benefitted even though he does not merit it. But it is not wrong to extend oneself further for a friend than for others, to work harder at serving his good, or to take risks for a friend that one would not take for others. The situation becomes very difficult when we consider cases such as remaining firm in one's support of a friend though one knows he is in the wrong. Such loyalty may be admirable and may prevent harm or injustice being done to one's friend. But it can also be blind, deriving its strength more from a kind of siege mentality and unreflective identification with the friend than from courage to stay with him through adversity. People do sometimes so strongly identify with friends as to regard a threat to them as a threat to themselves and to put the friendship before any other considerations. True friends *are* loyal, but not loyal no matter what. That would be incompatible with the best kind of friendships being based upon excellences of character.

In addition to unclarities about the relation of friendship to difficult moral cases, we also need to recognize that even sound friendships based upon virtue are not always, so to speak, at equilibrium. What Aristotle presents as a type of friendship is really more like an ideal at one end of a continuum. Friendships always involve nuances of personal chemistry, and they can be occasionally tempestuous or uneven, or at least involve types of agitation that need not undo them but do make the image of perfect friendship, composed of the elements of complete virtue and similarity of character, not quite representative of the real case.

We can of course also try to be good friends to weak or bad people, in the sense of encouraging them and supporting them in making themselves less weak or bad. Someone's poor character is not a license for ethically abandoning them and just writing them off. There is a difference, to be sure, between being friends with someone on a basis of equality, expecting loyalty and affection and participation in each other's lives, and befriending someone in order to help them, without them participating in your life. Some friendships with weak or bad people are of the latter type. We care about their good, strive to help them in understanding and achieving it, and do not want to dismiss them as incorrigible. In this sort of friendship, we are being good to them, or are at least trying to, not because of the good they exhibit but because of the good that we think is "in them" and that they deserve a chance to discover and enjoy. It is hard to be a friend to a really bad or weak person because they are likely either to put up resistance to our efforts or to try to grease the skids for us, worsening us by trying to get us to accommodate them or agree with them. Sometimes we are able to befriend persons who are weak or bad, though we cannot fully be friends with them because of the degree of inequality. We may give up on the job of doing good for them, finding it futile or too costly in a variety of ways. Perhaps their character is so firmly established that there is little reasonable hope of really doing good for them apart from wishing better for them. They are just hardened in their ways or unreceptive to the thought of changing their conception of what is worth doing. It is extremely difficult to know just when persons have crossed that sort of threshold and whether their crossing it is in part explained by the ways in which they are treated and regarded by others.

Kant says in his *Lectures on Ethics*, "Every one seeks to deserve friendship."[12] Certainly everyone wants friends, or if someone does not, an explanation of this extraordinary fact is called for. But Kant points out that people seek to *deserve* friendship. Friendship is an important good, and to have no friends is not only a lack but may very likely be accompanied by feelings of unworthiness. People often take considerable pride in their friends and feel as though it is a special good that they should have just those people as friends. Much can be learned about someone by considering who their friends are and what is the character of the bond of friendship. Some people want friends who are not only loyal to them but also honest, responsible people. Some people want friends who not only share many of their tastes and pleasures but are not vulgar or base or perverse. Whether or not someone wants human excellences in her friends shows a lot about her. Friends can be loyal, generous with each other, pleasing to each other, sacrifice for each other, and still be bad people. The fact that within a friendship people don't abuse, deceive, or mistreat each other is not itself proof of their soundness of character. Human beings can be remarkably selective in their moral concern. People of good character want friends of good character and believe that they deserve them. They believe this both in the sense that they believe they deserve friends who will not betray or otherwise ill-serve them and also in the sense that friends of good character confirm and appreciate and encourage one's own excellences.

FRIENDSHIP AND MORALITY

There is a kind of friendliness or good will that some people have towards others in general without knowledge of them. Some people are more disposed to be interested in others, to find them pleasing, and to be pleasing to them. This need not be just a matter of being good natured or sociable. It can reflect a character strong and sound enough to be a good judge of others, to be able to appreciate them and not hide behind defensiveness or suspicion or cynicism. This generalized friendliness is not a matter of doing good for others out of duty or just out of affect. It is a way of taking seriously people's welfare and recognizing their good as a reason for action. There are needs and interests that we have by virtue of being human and not on account of being me, you, or this one; we are capable of recognizing what is required for others' well-being, and we are capable of identifying with it to some extent. This is not always a matter of imagining oneself in the other person's position, though that may be part of it.

It is a matter of recognizing how fundamentally alike we really are in our nature and our predicament.

Generally we think of friendship as a close relation between individuals with knowledge of each other. Altruism we tend to think of more abstractly as a kind of concern we might have for anyone. Friendship entails knowledge of the individual in a way that altruism typically doesn't. Altruism often means acting for the sake of others just because they are in need or because one believes the good of others is worth protecting and promoting. It often does not involve personal feelings or concern in the way friendship does. For example, altruism may motivate in us the response to another's distress: "Someone should do something to help; indeed I should do something." In the case of a friend, we think, "I should do something," even if it never occurs to us that *someone* should do something. We are moved in a different way by the suffering of friends than by the suffering of others.

Our concern for others can be extended and animated by the kinds of concern we feel in friendship. It's not that altruism is an extension of friendship but that friendships can involve the kinds of relations and activities in which we develop concern for other persons and come to have a more articulate understanding of people's goods, needs, and interests. On the other hand, people often confine their moral concern to their friends. They may be honest, loyal, caring, and generous with them but unconcerned for and generally unwilling to do good for others. Friendship can teach virtue, but virtue can also be contracted to the circle of one's friends.

This is not to say that all of our moral concern should be impartial. Lawrence Blum, in *Friendship, Altruism, and Morality*, argues that "in normal contexts of friendship it is appropriate to act for the friend's benefit without having to vindicate that action from a perspective of impartiality."[13] He also argues that morality

> does not demand of us that we regard all our proposed actions from an impartial perspective. In this sense Kantianism fails to define "the moral point of view." For in areas of life in which impartiality is not applicable, other considerations will from a moral point of view be appropriate and valid. So it will be proper to act for the sake of one's friend's good simply as such, independent of the vindication of such action from an impartial point of view.
>
> This means also that friendship as a central human endeavor does not require a moral vindication, in the sense of a

> justification according to impersonal and universal principles. The personal importance which friendship has to us lies outside of this moral framework.[14]

Blum's point is that "in normal situations of comforting, helping, advising, sympathizing with, being concerned for, supporting, being glad for a friend, the impartial perspective is neither required nor appropriate."[15]

Blum is right to reject the claim that impartiality *defines* the moral point of view and also right to note how the moral validity of friendship surely does not depend upon impartiality. It is true that a great deal of ethics concerns the fact that something should be done by someone not because they are *that* person but because they are anyone who happens to be in those circumstances. It would be wrong to be selective in the exercise of our virtues, and an ethic without impartiality would be seriously deficient. But there is not a simple, exhaustive dichotomy between the impartial and the partial. Surely there is something morally excellent in acting for the sake of a friend's good, even though considerations of impartiality never arise. Friendship means taking seriously both the separateness and the individuality of the other person and also includes a kind of identification and sharing with him or her. We feel our own good to be bound up with the good of our friends. In this sense, as Price suggests, Aristotle's conception of friendship can dissolve "the obstinate dichotomy between egoism and altruism."[16] The good of our friends is a matter of genuine concern to ourselves, but not in an egoist way. A friend is a good to us, and so is the friend's well-being, but they are also goods that we recognize as having a standing outside of ourselves. This recognition is not a matter of principle or a matter of affect. It is the recognition of, desire for, and pleasure in the well-being of both ourselves and others. No one could be a friend strictly as a matter of principle, and friendships based solely on feelings of liking one another and finding each other's company pleasing are incomplete and more liable to dissolution than friendships based upon mutual knowledge and concern.

If friendship involves excellence of character and mutual knowledge, then it may seem a rare thing. On the other hand, it has been urged throughout that this is indeed the primary or most perfect kind of friendship. People have friendships of many kinds, some based more on personal "chemistry," some based more on character. It would be a serious error to ignore or discount the various kinds of imperfect friendships. Even the most excellent people will surely have some of those as well, and many people may have only friendships based upon mutual liking and interest or mutual utility.

In Blum's analysis, after criticizing the Kantian view for failing to adequately accommodate the moral dimensions of friendship, he goes on to say that there are different ways of overmoralizing it.

> One such view sees the concern for the friend's good as the central element in friendship, downplaying or neglecting the liking of the friend, the desire to be with him, the enjoyment of shared activities, etc.
>
> A second overmoralized view sees friendship, or at least the highest forms of it, as having its grounds, its object, or the source of connection between the friends primarily in the friend's moral qualities and character; Aristotle, for example, seems to hold this view in his discussion in *Nicomachean Ethics*. . . . One does not need to regard someone as a virtuous person in order to care for him as a friend; nor, in caring for him for his own sake need one focus primarily on whatever morally virtuous qualities he has.[17]

To an extent, this is surely right. But we can distinguish between morally excellent friendships, in which the mutual concern is based upon mutual knowledge and a concern for what is good, and friendships with a different character. And with Aristotle I would argue that the latter are, in important ways, lesser friendships. They may or may not seem incomplete to the people in them. Sometimes we really are aware of a lack of these things, sometimes not. It depends, in large part, upon how much we aim at them. This does not mean that in order to have friendships in the primary sense, people need to be able to lead lives of leisure and civic virtue, the kind of political life Aristotle talked about. And they certainly do not need a *theory* of human nature or human good or need to engage in systematic self-conscious reflection about such things. They need, however, to have a practical understanding of and concern for human good, a sense of the importance of certain needs being met and a sense of what makes some activities worthwhile and dignified and others not. They do not need to be heroically virtuous, but they must have soundness of character. Their excellence does not have to be revealed in acts that garner accolades, honor, or public attention; it only needs to be genuine. Virtuous activity need not mean striking exhibitions of virtue. Perhaps Aristotle's conception of the best friendships is somewhat overintellectualized and tailored to a conception of an excellent life in a quite specific type of community. These aspects need to be revised. But the core of it, excellence of character and practical wisdom, does not need much revision. His account of practical reason is ethical in the sense that he takes practical reasoning to be concerned with what is intrinsically good. All action aims at some good, and there can be better or worse understandings of what is worth aiming at. But while he sees a deep connection between virtue and practical reason in general, it is perhaps not quite right to say that he overmoralizes matters such as friendship. Rather, he appropriately recognizes them as ethically very significant.

Excellence of friendship does not require exceptional people or circumstances. What it does require is a stable disposition to do good for the other person for his or her sake and to enjoy doing it. And there surely are lasting, strong friendships and kinds of mutual concern that are not primarily grounded in moral qualities. The kind that is may not be the only or the most typical kind of friendship, but it is the most complete, and it has an ethical dimension that the other kinds lack. The sort of virtue that the best kind of friendship involves need not be extraordinary, and the relation certainly need not be between the great-souled. Many excellent friendships are based on mutual need and affection and a willingness to do good for each other without the parties to it being in any respects extraordinary. There is perhaps something particularly impressive about friendships between the great-souled, but that is because they involve the great-souled, not because they are superior friendships.

One of the things that is so important about friendship is that good friends love us for our character and encourage in us a sound sense of what is important. Good friends remind us when there is distortion or deception in how we think of ourselves, and they dissuade us from concerns and motives that waste our emotional energy. Friendship is a cause of self-love in that it helps us maintain a sense that we are worthy of the concern and affection of others and a sense of what it is about us that merits this. Good friends want to be good for each other and in so doing strengthen the bases of self-love. If we are honorable, people with practical wisdom will recognize that and appreciate it, and if they are our friends, they will love us for it and want us to love ourselves for it. Also, if people are not self-loving, it is less likely that they can enjoy the best kind of friendship. This is true in two ways. First, if we do not have the sort of character that is the appropriate ground of self-love, then we also are likely not to have the sort of understanding and appreciation of goods that are important to the best kind of friendship. Our judgments of worth and our commitments will not be of the sort that dispose us to encourage and enjoy excellence in others and welcome it as part of our own lives. Second, lack of self-love is often associated with suspicion, resentment, self-absorption, and other things that make sound friendship difficult. Also, self-loathing or feelings of unworthiness can hobble individuals for friendship, especially if they believe that they do not deserve to lead a flourishing life or that they could not be valued by others. They may very much want to overcome this but wonder if they can and if they deserve to. Others who make thoughtful, sustained efforts to be good to such people can strengthen their self-esteem and help them in becoming self-loving, and in so doing may become friends rather than just helpers. They can help those lacking in self-love to revise their self-conception and reorient their practical reasoning and sensibility. In this sense, they can enable persons to recognize abilities and possibilities and know themselves better through coming to know what they are capable of and recognizing that certain important goods are not inaccessible to them. Another's knowledge of oneself can be intimidating or motivate feelings of vulnerability. But it can also healthfully contribute to self-knowledge and self-love.

SELF-LOVE, FRIENDSHIP, AND PRACTICAL REASON

The discussion shows that there is a central role for practical reason and practical knowledge in both friendship and self-love, in terms of both supplying knowledge of good and organizing the activity of pursuing it. There *are* things for us to know about what it is good to desire and good to do, and the character of our activities is in large part consequent upon how reason figures in them. Moreover, the role of reason in this is not primarily to afford us knowledge of propositions. Its role is to organize desire and passion. Reason is that capacity which enables us to choose and act for ends, under concepts. This is one way in which love is not blind but can reflect knowledge. What is good is something that can be understood, not merely felt, and knowledge of it is needed in order for us to rationally desire it and to love it.

Practical reason is also what makes friendship and self-love *activities*. Neither of them is passive or a kind of feeling that just flows over us or wells up in us. One function of practical reasoning is not to disown or discourage feeling but to shape it into organized attitudes that figure in our judgments and motives. So, far from impoverishing or sequestering sensibility, reason integrates it into a unified personality in which understanding and feeling are in accord in imagination, receptivity, and purpose. We are best able to love ourselves and others when our sensibility and appetites and emotions are educated by reason. We thereby fashion habits of action that enable us to aim at good and to do so willingly and pleasingly. It is reason that shapes habits of *wanting* to act well, supplying to them their motive and goal.

The outside-in bias of Aristotle's account perhaps explains his apparent optimism—optimism about the possibility of knowledge of the good and consequent optimism about the similarity of virtuous individuals. There is a common human nature, and it and its good are knowable. They are not obvious or self-presenting, but perception and reflection can make them known. While habituation is necessary to prepare, so to speak, the soul for knowledge of its good by orienting the soul to it without knowledge, the object of this knowledge is common and objective.

These remarks point to a further matter, i.e., whether it is possible to be friends with persons from a very different setting. Their outlook, attitudes, and what they take pleasure in may be so different that there does not seem to be an adequate basis of commonality, of shared interest and judgments of worth, for friendship. This, I think, is easily and unhelpfully overstated. We should not harbor any illusions about people everywhere caring about just the same things in the same ways and the like. It is hard enough to be friends with one's next-door neighbor. Nonetheless, in spite of the varieties of tradition, aspiration, attitude, perspective, and so forth, it is immensely implausible to deny that there are goods, needs, and interests that are common and distinctively human and concern for which supplies a basis for friendship between people from even very different social or cultural settings. The problem is not that there are not considerations of these kinds but that people often use facts of difference as a basis for suspicion, resentment, animosity, or indifference. That, too, is to some extent distinctively human. In any case, knowledge is needed in order for a sound, enduring friendship to develop, both general knowledge and knowledge of the individual. Sometimes cultural or social differences make knowledge of the individual more difficult; sometimes they are what motivate seeking it. The differences between people may be what each person finds interesting about the other. Whether or not people from very different settings can be friends is not a philosophical matter. The bases for it exist in human nature. What the actual situations are and what people do in them are separate issues. There probably are not many—or even any—general laws or necessary truths about the extent to which people with quite different socially or culturally informed "second natures" can appreciate each other as human beings with a common nature. We do, however, know that they are able to. Practical reasoning can recognize goods across different social and historical settings, and it is not restricted by them.

Practical wisdom is not "local." It is an understanding of *human* good, and for all of the diversity of individuals and groups, it is their excellences as humans that we most value. Our nature as rational animals is what we are able to enjoy most stably and richly, in ourselves and others, and practical wisdom is our understanding of what is good in it and how to realize it.

Friendship and self-love are, at the same time, realizations of human good and are necessary for it, are both parts of and means to it. We *need* them in order to flourish, that is, to live in a way that is desirable for its own sake *because* it is a well-ordered exercise of human capacities, pleasing in itself. Friendship and self-love are ways of loving human nature through activity in accordance with knowledge of its good.

While friendship is an ethically significant relation and entails common conceptions of what is good, it is a relation individuals typically have with only a small number of people. This is, in large part, because of the knowledge of each other that it requires. There are several other ethically significant relations and types of concern for others, including compassion, altruism, and respect. These and friendship (and several others) need to be distinguished from each other, but they are also importantly interrelated. Friendship can instruct us in respect and altruism; compassion can be a beginning for friendship; a sound friendship involves mutual respect, and so forth. All of these are ethically crucial because they figure in our coming to understand others as human in the same sense as ourselves, with many of the same basic needs and interests.

In the following chapter, the focus shifts to on respect. This differs in quite important ways from friendship and self-love and plays a different role in moral motivation and relations between people. The main difference between it and friendship and self-love is that ethical respect is grounded in considerations about individuals as rational agents, rather than about an individual's particular qualities. This is a difference of focus and of emphasis, not a change of subject matter.

Respect, unlike friendship, is *owed* to people and is not dependent upon knowledge of them or upon specific shared conceptions of good. There are ethical constraints upon appropriate regard for and treatment of people that are not based upon sharing in the way that it figures in friendship but, rather, upon their rational nature and its likeness across persons. Kant was right in insisting that it is because persons are rational agents, because they are capable of self-determined action under concepts, that they are owed a certain distinctive regard and treatment. We take this up in the next two chapters.

CHAPTER 5

The Metaethics of Respect

For all of the variety of ethical realisms, they share this: they aim to reinvolve the world in morality, or at least aim to reinvolve something outside of the will and the passions. G. E. Moore sought to do this in terms of a real, objective, but undefinable property, good. Realist naturalists seek to do this by explaining values as supervenient upon natural and social facts. Wiggins, though not clearly a realist, seeks to explain moral judgment in terms of a coordination of response to property. Sabina Lovibond, a Wittgensteinian realist, writes that "objectivity, we have supposed, is a function of what Quine calls a 'pull' toward habits of judgment which are consistent with the adoption of a publicly accessible perspective on the world. Objective discourse is discourse in which, as a matter of logic, we cannot participate unless we are prepared to acknowledge certain intellectual authorities."[1] And she notes: "Our proposed theory of ethics, in short, is a realist theory in that it asserts the existence of *intellectual authority-relations* in the realm of morals, whereas non-cognitivism denies these."[2]

Realism seeks to reinstate perception, cognition, and the recognition of features of the world as a basis for action. Practical interest involves the understanding and is not the sole province of will, decision, or desire. We can *know* what to do and know it on the grounds that the world is a certain way or that there are certain things in it. Iris Murdoch, in *The Sovereignty of Good*, uses the idiom of "attention"[3] and "obedience to reality"[4] to articulate a version of realism according to which there is "the task of apprehending a magnetic but inexhaustible reality."[5] Subjectivity, personal fantasy, and volitions unguided by understanding are among the tendencies and doctrines that morality and moral theory need to overcome and reject, or at least strategically reinterpret. The realists argue that we do not create values by fiat or prescription or a will unguided by cognition. Our moral stances, policies, and judgments can and should be responses to the world, rather than the product of sensibility or decisions independent of cognition of it. Morality can be objective in a different sense than Kant wanted to make it by grounding it in principles he took to be rationally necessary. It can be objective by appreciating the significance of facts, properties, and features of an objective world.

What may seem somewhat paradoxical is that by denying the voluntarism and subjectivity of ethical noncognitivism, realism, in a way, *more* fully locates human beings in a normative order, a morally significant world. Nor is there a loss of moral freedom. Rather, ethical self-determination is to be understood in terms of not being misled or not being in ignorance or self-deceived; it is our ability to act on a true apprehension, to get the world and our action morally right. Our moral freedom is not alienated or diminished by reabsorption into a world we didn't make. Instead, moral realism is our way of being at home in the world by knowing it and thereby knowing our good. This, at least, is part of the point of practical realism. Self-knowledge depends upon a knowing engagement with the world. In order to decide rightly and act well (in the moral sense), we need to know the world of which morality is a dimension. Morality *answers* to something real.

This notion of answering to something real will be central to the account of respect here. Before going more fully into the issue of respect, a bit needs to be said about this notion of answering to something. In earlier chapters I argued that reason is practical in that it has a telos, that one employment of reason is to judge and choose in terms of good. The practical employment of reason is not altogether detached from passions and appetites, but as has been argued, ethical significance is an object of cognition, of practical thought. The telos of practical reason is, in one sense, the same as the telos of theoretical reason, namely, to answer to the world. In that respect practical reason is not merely a facilitator for desire or volition. This is not because there is one specific target that practical reason aims at but because there is a world that it refers to and operates in and on and that it needs to know in order to operate well. In practical reasoning we answer to the world, in the sense that it is an ethically significant world for practical reasoners. There are not value-entities, but there is a natural reality, which is the ethical realm we live in and can describe and respond to well or badly, with careful attention or with inattention, with concern to get things right or with ethical oblivion or deception. In trying to get this right, we are also achieving a better understanding of ourselves insofar as we are part of this world, must live in it, and through it try to find out our own good.

Antirealists sometimes charge realism with cutting us off from the world by taking the world to be external, over against us, and independent of our own thought and interests. And antirealists often hold that if their critiques of realist notions of reference and correspondence are right, then realism gives us skepticism and not the world: there is an unbridgeable gap between mind (or language) and the world, and if we try to build the bridge with realist materials, we stumble into the skeptic tank. As I argued earlier, it is antirealism, not realism, that is alienating. The right idiom for characterizing realism is not one that takes the world to be inaccessibly set over against us, foreign to us. It is, rather, one according to which cognitive activity is the actualization of the intelligibility of a world order it did not make. If anything, the appropriate idiom is one of recognition, not alienation, recognition of what is intelligible. Mind is a capacity for cognition, for conceptually actualizing what is intelligible. If we interpret mind as a capacity for cognition, as a capacity for actualizing intelligibility, then realism is not alienating because there is nothing for cognitive activity to be except in engagement with a reality that is not constituted by that activity. This is not the place to present the outlines of an overall theory of mind and world. But I suggest that the most satisfactory interpretation of their relation is one according to which, in order to know what mind does, we need to know what sort of reality it confronts. Its not being mind-constituted does not put it out of reach. Its intelligible features are what mind, in the activity of conceptualization and explanation, confronts, and responds to. And it is certainly an element of moral realism that practical mind responds, not primarily affectively but cognitively, to a reality the acknowledgment of which supplies reasons for action. The teleology of theoretical reason is to acknowledge what is encountered as reasons for belief. The teleology of practical reason is to acknowledge what is encountered as reasons for valuational judgment and action.

Metaphysical antirealism resorbs the objects of cognition into the activity of conceptualization and then, attending to that as not at any distance, claims that the reality of conceptualization is the reality confronted. It denies that in thinking about reality, we are just thinking about the activity of mind, but it abandons the metaphysical resources to sustain the claim. Cognitive states are not just acts of mind; they are actualizations, part of the causation of which is encounter with a real order that is not constituted by what mind thinks. Mind, in both its theoretical and practical activity, is informed by what it confronts. Otherwise, there is nothing for it to be true to. Mind is most at home in the world not by constituting it according to its own design (that would be just interior design) but by respecting it as what it is to answer to. Truth, realist truth, has authority in that it is the telos of cognitive activity.

Even if one insists that practical realism requires a human perspective, in the sense that it claims that reason doesn't discover and describe values "out there" but operates in a manner consequent upon conceptions of good, this is because reason in its practical exercise is cognition concerned with good. And our conceptions of good can be informed by facts independent of what our conative stances and valuational commitments are. Part of the point of practical realism is to re-engage us ethically to the world via the recognition that the interest of practical reason is to understand what is good by attention to the world.

An internal practical realism would have to interpret ethical notions in terms of ideals we construct, analogously to its interpretation of truth as idealized rational justification. But in both cases the absorption of the object into the system of cognition defeats the purpose of the latter insofar as it leaves us in a world of our constructions, rather than engaging us to a world that our conceptions answer to. We can recognize realist ethical significance, just as we can recognize realist causality or kind-membership; just as there are causal intelligibility and modal intelligibility discoverable in the world, so, too, there is ethical intelligibility. Our concepts render these things accessible, but what they render accessible is not determined by our concepts. Reason is a capacity for comprehension of the world both theoretically and practically.

RESPECT AND ATTENTION TO REALITY

A good deal of morality concerns actions for which there are rules or principles, such as those concerning making and keeping promises, repaying debts, the prohibition of theft, and so on. Many of these kinds of cases concern obligations that can be formulated fairly clearly, and they have to do with interactions between people that are in a sense legalistic or contractual, or at least require good faith and the reliability of one's word or agreement. But a good deal of morality is not like this. Even being fair to people—in what we say about them, how we regard them and act toward them—often involves some subtlety of judgment and recognition of facts about them (and ourselves) and their (and our) situations. For example, resenting someone's success and thereby being motivated to be vindictive or unkind is a way of being unfair. Denying someone a good they deserve or refusing them our sympathy because of their ethnic background is unfair. We can say that these are examples of violating moral rules, but that is a diagnosis that for some purposes is too abstract and arid. When we consider what is behind these moral failures and what is needed to overcome them, it is plain that this is largely a matter of attention to the ethical significance of quite specific facts, and of the ways in which selfishness or bias or insecurity, for example, distort our perception and corrupt our motives. Coming to realize the validity of a principle is often a matter of adjusting our attention to facts, bringing into proper focus what is ethically relevant, and being willing to let go of what isn't. Dealing with a difficult and emotionally charged situation involving friends or family, for example, is often not the sort of task that can be well done on the basis of appeal to principles. What is needed is depth and honesty in our formulation of what is at issue and a willingness to confront features of the circumstances that might be obscured by our desires or emotions. Our decision about what to do may instantiate a principle, but it will be arrived at by judgments that size up the situation and require attention to detail rather than derivation from principle.

This sort of attention, by which we take the world and people morally seriously, is an important form of respect. This is not respect in the sense of acknowledgment of a particular, fixed value. Rather, it is a disposition to look for, confront, and appreciate the moral significance of the facts. In many situations the main issue is not "What ethical principle applies?" but "What do these features of the situation count for?" The virtues, for example, are not only dispositions to act; they are intelligent dispositions to act because certain kinds of things are recognized. Practical wisdom is a kind of awareness as much as a readiness to act in certain ways. This is particularly evident when we consider situations that we are not directly involved in or in which, given our circumstances, we are not able to take action. Our ability to effectively describe and understand the ethical dimensions of characters, actions, and situations even where we are not the actors is reflective of our practical wisdom or lack of it.

Moral philosophy has appropriately focused on action, on doings, but the appropriateness of this should not drive out consideration of moral thought and imagination. Action is our main contribution to the world, but good action involves having understanding that is wider and more continuous than just the scope of our own actions. It needs a practical comprehension of the world that is not restricted to the exigencies of personal commitments or predicaments. Good ethical description and judgment (and, as a consequence, good action) are responsive to the features of the world that are the setting for action, the setting for the right fit of action in the world. But that fit depends upon what the world is like, and the goodness of action is not determinable by criteria independent of it.

This sort of attention to the world is not our attempt to apprehend an object, the good. For all of the affinity this discussion bears to Iris Murdoch's view in *The Sovereignty of Good*, it is a different view in important respects. For example, practical realism does not share her notion that "the image of the Good as a transcendent magnetic centre seems to me the least corruptible and most realistic picture for us to use in our reflections upon the moral life."[6] Nor does it share the notion that good has an "indefinable and non-representable character."[7] In attention to the world, we can come to know what we need to do (much of the time) and achieve right understandings of what in this or that situation is good to do and what, as a general matter, are excellences of character. These are not finite, inarticulate glimpses of a unitary, transcendent good that inspires pious obedience. The metaphysics of morals is a metaphysics of the world, a world susceptible to ethical description by practical reason. What practical realism does share with Murdoch's view is that there are things to know with respect to ethics, that what is good is not a matter of volition, and that it is through articulate, energetic, cognitive attention to the world that we find these things out, or at least have the best hope of doing so. But much that we find out is about ourselves, about orienting and regulating our passions and interests so that they are responsive to what reason can recognize.

One of the most important forms this attention takes is respect for human beings, an active and cognitive (not merely affective) concern to take human good seriously and to respond to practical reason's ethical comprehension of the world as a unified, moral world. We take this up directly in the next chapter.

CHAPTER 6

Realism and Respect

The task of this chapter is to explain why respect for persons is a central ethical notion and how it is accounted for by practical realism. The main claim is that it is respect for persons that unifies us in a common moral world. Not to respect people is a form of alienation from them and from objective good. To respect people is to acknowledge that they are equal participants in a common ethical world and that objective considerations of good are to direct our attitudes and actions. The realism of the view lies in its being grounded in a common human nature shared by participants in the ethical world. Proper ethical regard for them is not a subjective or optional matter. It does not properly depend primarily upon an extension of sympathy or the willingness or decision to participate in specific institutions or practices.

According to Kant, the categorical imperative could be equivalently formulated as a principle of respect. Persons, rational beings, exemplify the moral law, and on account of the rational self-legislation that enables persons to be moral agents, they have intrinsic value and are never to be treated merely as means. The Kantian notion is a useful one. It expresses the widely held notion that persons have a distinctive moral status and that they, as individuals, are to be regarded and treated in ways that are constrained by certain fixed limits. Kant grounded the principle of respect in practical reason. According to him, it is our practical rationality that makes us participants in a moral world and is the source of laws for that world.

This account, too, explains there being moral significance in the world on the basis of there being practical reasoners. But it explains this not in terms of formal features of practical reason but in terms of practical cognition. The notion that it is practical reason that makes it a morally significant world has an affinity with Kantianism. But the substance of the explanation is different. Before going into this more fully, we should at least mention some different approaches to the issue of what unifies the moral world.

MORAL UNITY

There are different kinds of accounts of what unifies people in a common moral world. One way to explain this is in terms of the extension of sympathy. Another is in terms of the (tacit) acceptance of conventions or the willingness to participate in certain institutions. These approaches are illustrated, respectively, by the positions of Bernard Williams in his *Morality: An Introduction to Ethics* and J. L. Mackie in his *Ethics: Inventing Right and Wrong*.

Williams argues that what is needed to get moral considerations "off the ground," what brings someone into the moral world, is the capability to think "in terms of other's interests" and that this is a matter of "sympathetic concern":

> If we grant a man even a minimal concern for others, then we do not have to ascribe to him any fundamentally new kind of thought or experience to include him in the world of morality, but only what is recognizably an extension of what he already has. . . .[1]

And

> It does not follow from this that having sympathetic concern for others is a necessary condition of being in the world of morality, that the way sketched is the *only* way "into morality." It does not follow from what has so far been said; but it is true.[2]

And according to J. L. Mackie moral requirements are not inescapable and the universalization of moral principles is not a matter of logic, such that failure to carry it through is indicative of irrationality. The special logic of morality is the special logic of a set of institutions that one may or may not endorse, and to fail to endorse them or to opt out of them are courses that practical rationality does not preclude. He argued that the acceptance of substantive practical principles is not required by logical or semantic considerations. "A logical or semantic truth is no real constraint on belief; nor, analogously, can one be any real constraint upon action or prescription or evaluation or choice of policy."[3] He argues for this view in his discussion of universalization, a discussion in which he concludes that engaging in moral thought as such does not commit one to any specific universalizable principles.

I will not undertake a discussion of Mackie's argument here. It is mentioned only to illustrate the position of a skeptic about what may be claimed to be the "intrinsic authority" of morality where this authority is traced to logical or semantic considerations.

Both the "extension of sympathetic concern" view and the "participation in institutions" view reject the notion that there are objective or realist grounds for the unity of the moral world. Each explains what it is to be in the ethical world in terms of (broadly) subjective considerations.

What I intend to capture and express by the notion of respect is both a requirement and an acknowledgment of something. In these senses, it is neither optional nor subjective. It may typically involve feelings of concern for others, but it is not a matter of feeling.

There are objective considerations of good that practical cognition understands. A general, stable disposition to guide action by that understanding is the manner in which respect for persons is actualized. The Kantian character of this respect, emphasized in one way by Nagel, is the regarding of oneself as one among others equally real and doing so in a way that acknowledges the objectivity of ethical considerations. But it is not the formal structure of practical reason that grounds respect. Rather, it is confrontation with the objective reality of ethical considerations, a reality that is not ego-dependent for its sense or significance. Respect is an acknowledgment of the authority and prescriptivity of practical truth. The disposition of respect is the disposition to respond motivationally to practical truth concerning intrinsic good.

Respect as a disposition of a practical reasoner is an active tendency to guide oneself by an understanding of practical truth. This unifies individuals in a common moral world, in that it is a manner of judging and deciding what to do on the basis of a concern to respond motivationally to the ethical significance of situations. Ethical significance is not ego-centered; it is not determined by a subject's interests or desires or sensibility. Ethical considerations are objective, impersonal, in the sense that what counts as an ethical consideration and the way it does so are a matter of cognition.

A person with good character may not even think in terms of respect as a specific principle or an explicit criterion of action, any more than they might think, "I should do this because this is the courageous thing to do." In fashioning institutional arrangements or establishing rules for a certain activity or practice, considerations of respect may enter into deliberation more explicitly. But in less formal dealings respect generally does not figure as an explicit consideration. It is nonetheless important.

A willingness to assist others without expectation of reward and just for the reason that they need help and you are able to help is a form of respect. Fulfilling one's responsibilities in a thorough and honest manner is a form of self-respect and also respect for others who depend upon the tasks being well done. In these and other contexts, the idea that one has any special obligations to particular individuals may not enter into a decision. Certainly one may do the right things for the right reasons without taking this to be a matter of duty. In acting for ethical reasons, the agent may have no awareness of doing what is a duty but, rather, be responding to the realities with a disposition to be clear about their ethical significance and to see through what is called for. This may not involve any self-conscious thought of considerations *as* ethical. If good dispositions are firmly established and acting from them is second nature, the judgment or decision that is ethically required need not be consciously sorted out from other possibilities. The agent's cognitive and affective engagement with the situation may be determinative of judgment without the agent having to identify and reject alternatives. The recognition of ethical significance and motivationally responding to it can carry through action without having been victors in a battle with inclination or the ego.

In claiming that the fundamental principle of morality could be expressed in a formula concerning respect for persons, Kant was right in assigning to respect centrality and generality. The explication of it, though, does not depend upon an a priori metaphysics of persons being ends in themselves. That there are objective considerations of ethical good is adequate for it.

Still, it is important to ask why it is that persons are objects of respect, why individual human beings are owed a distinctive kind of regard. We argued earlier that human beings are capable of rational motion, of action guided by conceptions of worth. The behavior of some other kinds of creatures can often be explained in terms of the attribution of beliefs and desires to them, but only human beings act with a view toward goods that they conceptualize, give reasons for, and criticize. Moreover, human beings can direct their action by considerations of objective good. Ethically, this counts for something. We should consider Kant's view and some descendants of it in order to clarify the contrast with the present view. Kant argued that rational beings are ends in themselves.

> Now, I say, man and, in general, every rational being exists as an end in himself and not merely as a means to be arbitrarily used by this or that will. . . .
>
> Beings whose existence does not depend on our will but on nature, if they are not rational beings, have only a relative worth as means and are therefore called "things"; on the other hand, rational beings are designated "persons" because their nature indicates that they are ends in themselves, i.e., things which may not be used merely as means. Such a being is thus an object of respect and, so far, restricts all [arbitrary] choice.[4]

Only persons are intrinsically valuable, and never to be valued merely as means. So, according to a Kantian view, whatever it is about persons that we might esteem or respect them *for*, there is a distinctive kind of regard owed to them just because they are persons, and this is a matter of rational principle, a requirement on us, whatever else we happen to value or want.

Alan Donagan summarizes the Kantian notion that humans are ends in themselves as follows: "We are self-governing, at bottom, because our rational agency entails that we are negatively free—that our actions are not causally determined by anything, such as instinct or desire, which is external to reason. Our negative freedom grounds our status as ends in ourselves. And that status furnishes the content of the fundamental principle of morality."[5]

Our being autonomous cannot be demonstrated, and thus it cannot be demonstrated that persons are to be respected as ends in themselves. But Kant did believe that his conception of human action and the morally relevant dimensions of practical reason supported this notion of unconditional respect, not just as an appealing ideal but as compelling. Reflection on what it is to be a practical reasoner yields the principle that a practical reasoner is to be respected because such a being legislates for itself and is no mere object or producible end. Any other end can be judged and can be rejected or abandoned; but an end in itself is a fixed limit for practical reason.

The role of this in Kant's ethics is central. Because of what persons are (and not because of what they are like), we have certain obligations to them. This all turns on reason. Persons are intrinsically valuable because as rational beings they are capable of "acting according to the conception of laws, i.e., according to principles."[6] Their rational causality is to be respected; and it is to be respected because it is a capacity to legislate principles valid for all rational beings. The ground of respect for others and the ground of self-respect is the same; it is this capacity for fully rational willing. Respect is not a feeling for another, and it is not based on sympathetic identification or empathy.

To respect persons is to respect the moral law; to act on maxims that are universalizable by rational beings. The ground of this respect is the self-legislation of rational agency. The form it takes is the universalizability of maxims. Respect is an ideal, but it is an ideal grounded in the very condition for morality, the capacity to act under the conception of law. Respect, law, freedom, and the notion of an end in itself are parts of a metaphysical package, each of which is explanatorily related to the others in a way that indicates how it is possible for there to be morality and what is its general character.

Nagel's approach in *The Possibility of Altruism* generates a principle of respect, but not from a basis in noumenal freedom. Like Kant, he is concerned to show that there are objective moral principles, and like Kant, he is concerned to show that ethical requirements have a source in the structure of practical rationality. He does not rely on a distinction between obligation and inclination in the way that Kant does. Kant's metaphysical version of the two standpoints is replaced by Nagel with the distinction between conceptualizing oneself as "I" and also, impersonally, as "someone," one among other selves equally real. But neither conceptualization is optional, and Nagel maintains that the unity of the self can only be retained by acting on objective reasons. Only objective, impersonal principles enable one to avoid practical solipsism, in which one cannot attach the same sense to reasons for oneself and for others. Consequently, subjective principles "do not warrant judgments or attitudes with motivational content concerning acts or states of affairs viewed impersonally."[7] And when from one standpoint we "cannot accept the judgments of the other, we are faced with a situation in which the individual is not operating as a unit. Two sides of the idea of himself, and hence two sides of himself, are coming apart. The only principles which avoid this result in the practical sphere are objective ones."[8] Like Kant, who insisted that the two standpoints were united in one subject, Nagel undertakes to show that the personal and impersonal standpoints are parts of a unity, a unity held together by structural features of practical reason.

So, while Kant argues that persons are owed respect because of their rational agency, because of their autonomy, Nagel says that "the requirement of objectivity demands that full weight be accorded to the distinction between persons, and to the irreducible significance of individual human lives, when the interests of different individuals are to be weighted against one another in a calculus of objective reasons."[9] And he refers to this claim as expressing "respect for individuals."[10]

The separateness of persons has, of course, also been centrally employed as a principle by Rawls. And while neither Rawls nor Nagel relies on Kant's theory of noumenal personality, the continuity between the three theories is plain. Objective considerations of rational endorsability require that persons be respected as individuals. The Nagel and Rawls accounts are worked out without explicit commitment to the Kantian notion of persons as ends in themselves. But the appeal to formal features of practical reason has a definite and significant affinity with it.

Donagan is more willing to make a direct appeal to the notion of an end in itself. Kant did not, he says,

> demonstrate a priori that reason must by its very nature prescribe for free and rational beings what the fundamental principle of morality says it must. Rather he drew attention to certain characteristics implicit in being a rational creature, with regard to which he claimed to have sufficient insight into the nature of practical reason confidently to affirm that it must prescribe that rational creatures be unconditionally respected.[11]

Rational nature is a nonproducible end, no mere object of desire. It is a nature that determines for itself a law, a principle of action, and "as an end to be respected, by virtue of which things are to be done, it can generate action."[12]

Whether the concern is the avoidance of practical solipsism (Nagel), the construction of principles of justice (Rawls), or an explication of how a rational creature is an end in itself (Donagan), Kantian resources have been deployed to show that there is a distinctive kind of respect owed to persons. And these resources refer to features of practical reason. It seems as though for nonskeptics about practical reason, for theorists who maintain that reason can be practical, respect for persons figures as a fundamental moral requirement.

This is not the case for Aristotle, however, even though he, too, held that reason can be practical. But in Aristotle's case, reason is practical because practical reasoning determines and directs us toward the proper object of desire. To reason practically is to determine for action its proper object, to inform desire by cognition. This is a somewhat different metaphysic of practical reason and, I believe, a more plausible one. The Kantian approach considers reason alone as a cause of action and as a determinant of principles of action. Desire and reason are distinct sources of motivation and distinct origins of ends of action. It is this sort of dualism that we have argued is problematic. It really is obscure how reason alone could perform either of the functions thus assigned to it. Human beings do act for ends, do so for reasons, and are capable of assessing and responding to the assessment of reasons. In that sense, it is plain that reason is practical, though for it to be practical, it need not be autonomous in the Kantian manner.

We are, as Aristotle held, purposive beings because we are beings to whom desire is essential. As we explained in chapter 1, this does not mean that the ground of motivation is nonrational. Nor does it mean that the ends of action are supplied from a nonrational source. Many of the goods human beings aim at are goods that are judged to be worthy of being actualized. They are not all simply independent producible ends given by desire. And actions that are good in themselves are also good *for* people. Acting courageously or honestly or justly is conducive to needs being met and well-being being promoted. And courage, honesty, and justice are virtues because of how they figure in human beings leading good lives. Even when concern for outcomes is important, it is not that the agent happens to desire them that makes them good. It is their being understood to be good that makes them objects of action.

The Aristotelian view can support an account of respect owed to persons as a basic moral requirement, and it can do so as part of a moral psychology that is more compelling than the Kantian one. A human being is a locus of good activity, and it is for the sake of human good that ethical action is undertaken. To respect persons is, in part, to be disposed to respond to objective considerations of good. Respect excludes treating or regarding people merely as means, and it entails acting for reasons that other rational agents would recognize as justifying. To respect people is to acknowledge their full and equal inclusion in ethical life, in an ethically significant world. This is not determined by structural features of practical reason ascertainable a priori. Rather, it is consequent upon cognitive recognition of the ethical significance of human nature.

The individual with practical wisdom respects others out of active engagement with what is good for human beings, and also takes pleasure in the actualization of good. When we have respect as a disposition, we enjoy the fact that justice is served, that others are not suffering, that we have done right by others. Respect is a generalized, practical concern to see good realized. It is not owed to persons because each individual has intrinsic worth but because it is in the lives of persons that objective, intrinsic good is realized. If a person loves what is ethically good, this is exercised as a respectful concern for people. Malice, contempt, cruelty, and the like include acknowledging the reality of others but in such a way that their failure, frustration, or suffering is what is enjoyed, rather than their good. Respect does not require affection or special concern for this or that individual, but it does require generalized concern for the good of people. A lack of respect is indicative of a failure to appreciate and take seriously in a practical manner the objectivity and generality of ethical considerations.

RESPECT AND RESPONSIBILITY

Practical reasoners are causes, causes of their own action, and they act in accordance with their own conceptions of worth. Part of respecting persons is regarding them as responsible agents, acknowledging them as origins of action. If someone is very bad and acts very badly, he or she forfeits esteem, admiration, trust, and so forth. But such people are to be no less respected as agents, in the sense of regarding them as accountable. In the absence of coercion and other kinds of excusing conditions, individuals are responsible for their actions, for their undertaking to make real their conceptions of what is worth doing. This kind of respect need involve no sort of honorific regard. It can be accorded to a person who is loathsome on account of his vices and also to a person who exhibits weakness or lack of resolve. Failure to respect someone as a responsible agent is failure to fully respect him as a human being, even if our judgment of him is harsh. But even a harsh judgment is symptomatic of the range of expectations and the sorts of norms of action reasonably applied to a human being as an origin of action. Often respecting persons requires of us that we act in ways that they do not think good, because they do not understand what is good or because of corruptions of character. A concern for human good is not the same as a concern for what pleases people. It is a disposition to do what is good, in the sense that it is ethically required.

Human action is, most of it, voluntary. And much of that voluntary action is rational motion, motion given its sense and point by choice or decision, even if there has been no conscious or articulate process of deliberation. This is the basis of responsibility for action. The decisions that issue in action are not only decisions that are one's own, they are exercises of one's causality as an agent acting on conceptions of worth. These are not necessitated or innate or beyond the control of the individual. That they are not is part of what makes the individual an agent. Even if it seems that Aristotle's argument for our being responsible for our own character and for what appears good to us seems too strict a line to take, one's actions typically are one's own in that the individual is the origin of them; they are contingent and up to the individual, and they are an actualization of what the person thinks good. For all the causal influence of upbringing, habit, and so forth, it is *we* who perform actions, and those actions are contingent in their being up to us; they are not simply causal consequences of prior events or forces or circumstances. They are acts original to us as conscious, deliberating, voluntary agents.

Whatever causal story might be told about why an individual does *that*, or does that instead of some other thing, the starting point for ethical consideration is that *that* individual did it, or plans to, or can, and in the absence of coercive or compulsive factors. It is the agency of the individual that is decisive to the doing. The individual is not just an element in a causal process uniform in the nature of causality at work. There are sometimes excusing conditions or extenuating factors, and always a complex variety of biological, social, and other causal factors at work on us. But our basic notions of voluntariness and responsibility are shaped by the fact that the natural order includes certain beings for whom what they do is "up to" them: their doing it can be directed by their own choosing, and an action's being up to them is not a matter of something happening "through" them but, rather, of it only happening at all on account of their being the origin of it. These are elements of practical understanding of the world and not initially results of theorizing about causation, laws, or modality. The human world is a practical world, a world of individuals performing actions that they are responsible for because they move on the basis of their own notions of what to do and their actions are initiated by them, not as steps in a process going on anyway, but as motion original to the agent.

In the traditional debate of free will versus determinism, the divide over whether it is the causal story or the exercise of contracausal agency that accounts for action is one of the most familiar features. The view here is not an endorsement of any specific theory of the will as an agent-cause or part of one. In our moral and legal concern with action, we are generally interested in both the story and the fact that a particular individual did such and such. That fact does not render the story nugatory, and neither does the story eliminate the significance of that fact. If someone has robbed several convenience stores and terrorized employees and customers each time, we are interested in both the fact of their voluntarily doing this and the story of why they do it. These interests pull in seemingly different directions, and this difference cannot just be smoothed over with a blanket endorsement of compatibilism. The causal-story side of compatibilism reflects a different kind of interest from the responsible-agency side. The former regards the act as an event occurring in an overall causal system; the latter regards it, more fundamentally practically, as an undertaking enacting a person's conception of what it is good to do. It won't do just to assimilate this into beliefs and desires operating as causes. It is *that individual,* that human being we take to be responsible, in part because we take people to be (to some extent and typically) responsible for what they think good to do. The question "What caused you to engage in that behavior?" is not always just a different but equivalent formulation of the question "Why do you think it's all right to do that sort of thing?"

This is not to say that theorizing about causation, laws, and modality can not be brought to bear on this practical notion of human action. But, in addition to whatever may seem satisfactory on these sorts of grounds, there remains this practical understanding of action and responsibility, one that arises in the familiar context of acting and doing and responding to the actions of others. Whatever we know about the laws of nature, the human world remains a practical world, a world given its contour and significance by our being sources of action and directing our own action. Taking human beings to be voluntary and responsible agents is part of recognizing them as human. It is individual human beings enacting specific values that are the agents of the practical world, the appropriate objects of ethical concern, and the appropriate subjects of ethical responsibility.

A great deal of our interaction with each other turns on this fundamentally practical appreciation, an appreciation by which we take each other to be not only appropriate objects of praise and blame or admiration and condemnation but also amenable to influence and persuasion. Here influence or persuasion is not primarily a matter of adjusting causal variables but of addressing and appealing to an individual as an agent, as a source of rational action.

Part of respecting human beings is acknowledging them as agents responsible for their actions; or, to put the point differently, because people are origins of their actions and generally responsible for them, respect for them is merited. By respect here I mean that it is appropriate to regard and treat each human being as a locus of rational action, and our concern is not just with the outcome of action but with the agent of it as a participant in an ethical order. Everybody has a "story," but a human being is not just a vehicle of that story, enacting it without any original control or direction. Our knowledge of what we intend and do and our capacity to imagine and consider alternative ends and means enable us to exercise authorship over many of our actions, and it is this which is appropriately admired and deplored about good and bad action respectively, both in a self-referring manner and with regard to others.

RESPECT AND SELF-RESPECT

In Kant's moral philosophy, one way in which respect is important is as rational reciprocity; respect is the rational formula through which an individual acknowledges that good reasons are not ego-centered. The respect that rationality elicits entails seeing morally valid principles as universal. Practical realism explains objectivity differently. To respect human beings is to recognize and to take seriously in practical reasoning that there are goods for practical reasoners constituted as we are and capable of voluntary action. Part of respecting a child, for example, is recognizing that she needs to develop abilities for rational self-determination and that the child does so, in large part, by being habituated to pay attention to certain kinds of things and to learn to take responsibility. Indeed, learning respect is an important part of moral education. Young people can be habituated in ways that dispose them to attend to what is ethically significant. Moreover, a child's propensity to imitate and her willingness to trust her parents can be encouraged in the direction of wanting to act well. If a parent is self-respecting and acts well, it is much more likely that the child will be the same as a matter of second nature. In both seeking and responding to the authority of adults, children are guided by example and can come to want the right sorts of things. Learning to be unselfish, to cooperate, to be honest, patient, and fair, and so forth, are the ways in which ethical significance is disclosed and the ways in which people learn to respect themselves and others. While this is a matter of habituation early on, it is the manner in which a young person is prepared to be attentive to the right things and to be able to reason about them. Part of respecting the child or younger person is appreciating the fact that she will emulate adults she is close to and that she will become like them. Another aspect of it is enjoying the development of ethical dispositions in the child. Values are transmitted without formal teaching. Being an example of virtue is much more important, since it literally shapes the practical world. Thus, taking responsibility for the transmission of values is a way of showing respectful concern for what sort of person the youngster will become.

Part of respecting adults is making allowances for their own individual desires and concerns and choices while still expecting of them self-control and fulfillment of reasonable norms of accountability and practical understanding. Except in extraordinary circumstances, we appropriately expect people to have both acceptable ideals and conceptions of worth and also good sense and a measure of fortitude in acting on them. And we reasonably expect people to be capable of revising their conceptions of what is good to do. We can listen to and respond to criticism and reflect on what sorts of people we are and what difference our own choices and actions make to this. We understand the human world as a context given point and coherence by ideals, policies of action, and grounds for them that we have responsibility for on account of reason.

The point is not that a human being has some distinctive kind of intrinsic value but that it is a feature of well-ordered practical reason to exhibit concern for objective moral value and that value is actualized in the lives of human beings. A practical reasoner is someone for whom there are objective considerations of value and for whom certain kinds of activity can be judged intrinsically worthwhile. In respecting people we exercise practical concern to promote human good and the enabling conditions for it.

This concern takes the form of recognizing limits on interference in another's life and also recognizing reasons for aiding and cooperating with people in a variety of ways. If we abandon someone in distress because we are vengeful on account of some earlier slight, it is plain that our act is wrong, but we don't need a theory of rights to show this. If we take advantage of someone's submissiveness and accustom them to doing things that a more fully self-respecting person wouldn't do, that, too, is a failure of respect and is understood to be such independently of specific rights-claims. We might try to work up into rights-claims any number of moral considerations, but their legitimacy will be derivative from a wider, less formalized understanding of the respect owed to people. What McDowell has called uncodifiability is true of respect as well as of other aspects of morality, such as the virtues. The situations to which moral concepts apply are too numerous in variety, too rich in the peculiarity of detail to be a basis for "a mechanical application of rules."[13] Lying to someone for malicious sport is a failure of respect; so is regarding someone else's difficulties or their suffering mainly as an inconvenience to oneself. And so is failing to show any concern for what sorts of motivations someone has and why. A failure of respect need not be malicious or involve interfering with persons in a direct way. It may be a matter of not bothering to acknowledge them as responsible, voluntary agents and regarding them instead just in terms of what difference to us or our concerns is made by what they do. But these are not all failures of respect in exactly the same way. There is not some single high-level rule that they all violate.

Respect is exhibited through the making of careful judgments on the basis of close attention to situations. It often entails trying to understand more fully the facts of people's circumstances and making decisions that address individuals as individuals, showing concern for their good. Doing so is not an alternative to being fair or impartial, it is a way of being fair and impartial. Concern for specifics is not an entryway for special pleading or a suspension of impartiality. It is the attention to the realities of situations that enables us to act in ways that are appropriately calibrated to the details of life. Acknowledging someone's special needs and taking seriously the conditions that impede someone's fulfilling her responsibilities are ways of respecting her as an individual. Treating people as full and equal participants in an ethical world often requires us to look carefully at what is required by quite particular circumstances. Often it does not, and highly general considerations of good action are then what make for respect. But the unity of the moral world is sustained by situation-specific appreciation of what is required. An engagement to good as the objective of practical reasoning can not be actualized and upheld just by a disposition to follow general rules.

Universalizability is a way of expressing the truth that respect is owed to persons, but is not the basis of it. In "Universalizability, Impartiality, Truth" D. Wiggins says that universalization "is no longer a method or any part of a method for the initial generation of moral ideas and principles. It works on what is already fully moralized and in no way merely *prima facie*. At best, it is a method of reminder and adjustment *already implicit* in what it is deployed upon."[14] The universalizer, he says, is "not in the role of an explorer or first map-maker but in the role of a surveyor visiting a scene already discovered and directly known."[15] What, in the present view, the method of universalization is "deployed upon" are the products of practical cognition: notions of well-being, harm, fairness, what is in a person's interest, what is desirable and why, what can be expected of a human being as an agent, the appropriateness of attributions of accountability, the ability to know what one is doing and what it ethically counts for. Universalization can adjust, interconnect, and put into the form of principles many considerations of these kinds, or at least can see to what extent they can be generalized.

While there are some valid generalizations about morally respecting people (of particular importance is that they are not to be treated merely as means, that their self-determination is to be encouraged, that they are to be regarded as having equal moral status), what constitutes respecting someone depends upon the details of the situation. We can respect a child by teaching him that there are reasons to act in some ways rather than others, and we can respect an adult by expecting him to both know what many of these reasons are and to act on them. Sometimes respecting a person requires us to extend ourselves even to interfere with another (if they are overcome with despair or anxiety and are contemplating something self-destructive). Sometimes it requires us to back off and leave someone to his own judgment and allow the responsibility for action to be his own. What we bring to a situation in respecting the people in it is not an a priori rule definitive of morality but perception, conceptualization, and an aspiration to achieve a true ethical description that can guide action.

Respect for oneself has the same basic grounds as respect for others. It is a concern for oneself as a practical reasoner, a concern for the integrity of one's practical reasoning and the soundness of one's values and character. Someone who is self-respecting enjoys acting well and recognizes excellences of character as desirable for their own sake. Self-respecting persons aim to bring their desires into agreement with practical understanding. They find it pleasurable to act in ways that are informed by practical truth. They enjoy acting from ethical dispositions as a confirmation of the values they engage with, and they aspire to sustain those dispositions. Being self-respecting, like being self-loving, is a natural and normal condition of a human being, in that it is a right appreciation of one's significance as a practical reasoner. It is not exactly the same as self-love, however. The latter is an achievement, the former more a regulative concern, a kind of attention to one's responsibilities as self-determining and as actualizing conceptions of worth. Self-respect is a recognition that it is important that one's choices, purposes, and policies of action answer to a sound conception of what is good. It is also the acknowledgment that what one does makes a difference to who one is, that responses and choices shape dispositions and are not unconnected episodes without influence on character. Persons who lack self-respect as a regulative concern do not give proper thought to what good activity and a good life mean, and are satisfied with either aggrandizing their ego, or indulging their appetites and passions, or ignoring the generality and objectivity of considerations of human good. They don't recognize the latter as grounds of categorical requirements, as considerations for guiding their own rational causality. For self-respecting persons, weakness of will is painful, and there is a motive to bring themselves into their "normal" state, to possess excellences of character and enjoy them. Analogously to persons maintaining their biological health through good habits and good judgment, we can maintain our self-respect through engagement with what we correctly understand to be good with reference to action. The idea that there are norms for the exercise of one's causality is the core of self-respect. It is not autonomy, in the sense of spontaneous self-legislation, that is crucial; it is the fact that one's causality as an agent can realize intrinsic value and that this is a capacity enjoyed because it is an excellence of our nature.

RESPECT AND ALIENATION

I argued previously that ethical realism is not only not alienating, it is what practically engages us to the world. Respect is what practically engages us to other people. By respecting people, we participate responsibly in a normative order; by failing to respect people, we are alienated from objective considerations of good and alienated from other people. Earlier we briefly characterized subjectivist approaches to unifying the moral world, and a few pages ago we took a brief look at Nagel's argument that only objective, impersonal principles of practical reason can overcome practical solipsism, which is alienation, a kind of dissociation, a failure to see that objective considerations of value are authoritative for us.

In *The Possibility of Altruism,* Nagel argues that "ethics is a struggle against a certain form of the egocentric predicament, just as prudential reasoning is a struggle against domination by the present,"[16] and that "the avoidance of dissociation therefore requires the acceptance of universal practical principles which apply in the same sense to everyone, and which are impersonally formulable."[17] Murdoch, in *The Sovereignty of Good,* comments that "in the moral life the enemy is the fat relentless ego."[18] She remarks how rare it is to find in someone the absence of "the anxious avaricious tentacles of the self."[19] The struggle against the self is interpreted differently by the two authors, Nagel explicating it as a person's seeing himself as one among others and Murdoch as directing attention to a transcendent Good and away from fantasy, self-centeredness, and voluntarist value-creation. As different as these interpretations are, both are motivated by a concern for objectivity in ethics, and objectivity is undermined when practical thought is contracted to the promptings of the ego. Nagel responds with structural considerations about practical reason, Murdoch with an appeal to a supersensible reality to which genuine virtue is obedient. For Nagel, respecting persons means acting on objective practical principles impersonally conceived. For Murdoch, on the other hand, "one of the most difficult and central of all virtues" is humility, "selfless respect for reality."[20]

Their emphasis on the ego as an agent of ethical disorientation is well placed but perhaps exaggerated. Part of the thrust of realism is that in addition to its being nonegoistic in its conception of good, it is cognitivist. In subjectivist or projectivist theories, there is an inadequate account of the unity of the moral world, not because they are based upon egoistic considerations but because they do not have the resources to explain how the interests of others can be a ground for categorical requirements. The problem is not that they take the self to be the determiner of good but that they leave concern for good a matter of sensibility that does not and cannot answer to considerations that have rationally informed prescriptive authority. In acting badly it may often be the ego that is accountable. But the general issue of what it is that locates us in an ethical order in the first place is not primarily a matter of overcoming egoistic tendencies. Acting well often requires this. But what constitutes the human world to be ethically significant is that we can act from an understanding of objective good. And the object of this understanding is the common human world. Not to recognize this is to be alienated from others, insofar as it is a way of limiting the sense and significance of considerations of good to an artificially restricted constituency. Cognition of good has a logical reach that sensibility and subjectivity do not; or at least their extension is only accidentally universal.

Granted, if we list defects of character, many of them include the self by name; self-absorption, self-importance, self-righteousness, self-centeredness, for example. And moral defects and weaknesses can almost always be described in ways that implicate the self. But it would be somewhat misleading to diagnose the issue only in terms of the self versus morality, and descriptions can be usefully broadened in the idiom of subjectivity and objectivity, knowledge and error, clarity and unclarity, weakness and resolve, and so forth. These are not all just variants of a single dualism, and enough texture needs to be included in order not to make the terms of analysis too narrow. Having morally sound judgment and good character entails overcoming tendencies to self-centeredness, but there are ways of succumbing to appetite or passion or of failing to attend and judge accurately that are not primarily attributable to those tendencies. A person's moral outlook and range of concern can be narrow or misguided or simplistic because of a lack of fluency with ethical concepts or a lack of subtlety in making ethical judgments that are not the result of "the fat relentless ego" gorging on self-aggrandizement.

If we understand an agent as a being with reason and desires for whom good action is shaped by desire informed by reason, we are less inclined to interpret bad action in terms of interference of the ego as the main problem. Rather, the main issue is the agent's understanding of good and the extent to which it is credentialed by reason and acted on through his own initiative. Acting for the sake of the apparent good rather than real good is not mainly a matter of egoism, though it often is virtually the same as privileging oneself with respect to others. The problem is often error, ignorance, or defect of character more than it is egoism.

If it is true that realism does not require an infinite, transcendent reality to explain objective value and if it is true that a conception of practical reason is not independent of its objects, then practical realism is well equipped to explain the ethical defects of alienation or dissociation and why individual human beings are owed a distinctive kind of respect on the basis of facts about their nature. For practical reasoners can appreciate the world as morally significant because they can understand what facts and situations count for in objective conceptions of good and they can act on those conceptions. If moral reasons depend upon an agent's subjective motivational set or if they depend upon what the norms and conventions of a group happen to be, then there are no objective, cognitivist grounds for respecting persons. In the latter case there may well be an "institutional" reality that is prescriptive—a set of practices, expectations, and criteria of good action that are objective for the participants insofar as they constitute what counts as this or that sort of action and what counts as having done it appropriately or well. But even if these are universalized, their universality will be consequent upon decisions and endorsements, rather than upon the generality of realist considerations.

RESPECT AND INESCAPABILITY

Earlier we took note of Mackie's denial that either logic or semantics necessitates the acceptance of any substantive practical principles. This comes in his discussion of universalization; it is part of his examination of whether the use of moral language or concepts determines any practical requirements. He diagnoses three stages of universalization in order to see if there is some interpretation of universalization that is rationally inescapable and yields significant moral content. After considering the first stage, at which numerical differences are ruled out as irrelevant, and the second stage, at which one puts oneself in the other's place, he reaches the third and final stage, which "rules out differences which answer to particular tastes, preferences, values, and ideals."[21] While this stage, he says, owes the least to subjectivity and can be pressed to the point of "equal account of all actual interests,"[22] one's adoption of principles satisfying the demands of this stage of universalization remains a matter of decision. "It is not only logically possible to opt out of this third variety of moral language game; it is quite common and conventional for people with strong moral convictions to remain outside it, and it may well require a conscious decision to opt into it."[23] There is nothing intrinsically compelling, nothing rationally irresistible about either the substance of moral principles or the logic of universalization. Conventions can be enforced, and people may adopt and sustain principles with conviction; but they do not have any objective necessity.

According to Harman, there are moral facts only relative to conventions, and there are moral reasons only given the acceptance of certain conventions.[24] Someone ought morally to do something only if there is a reason for that person to do it, and whether there is a reason and what it is are matters of "tacit convention."[25]

Both Harman and Mackie reject the view that moral claims can be objective in the sense that they refer to or are based upon cognitively accessible features of the world, the understanding of which is ethically prescriptive. Both reject realism about moral considerations and objective prescriptivity.

We can agree that an a priori rational command is not a sine qua non of morality and that practical principles and their prescriptive authority are not consequences of moral language. Where practical realism cannot agree with the alternatives mentioned is in their denial that there are cognitive, prescriptive considerations for moral judgments to answer to. In the issue of respect, this contrast is particularly clear. We can not simply take it for granted that human beings are equal participants in the moral world, nor can we make them such by convention or prescription. Or perhaps we could, but there would always be both logical and moral space to opt out. For the realist, respect is an inescapable element of morality. It is not irresistible, since obviously people can and do fail to respect others. But it inescapable in the sense that the reality that practical reason takes as its object is a sufficient justifying ground for it. It is morally but not logically or psychologically inescapable. On the issue of inescapability, Philippa Foot writes:

> No one, it is said, escapes the requirements of ethics by having or not having particular interests or desires. Taken in one way this only reiterates the contrast between the "should" of morality and the hypothetical "should," and once more places morality alongside of etiquette. Both are inescapable in that behaviour

> does not cease to offend against either morality or etiquette because the agent is indifferent to their purposes and to the disapproval he will incur by flouting them. But morality is supposed to be inescapable in some special way and this may turn out to be merely the reflection of the way morality is taught.[26]

Moral judgments, argues Foot, "have no better claim to be categorical imperatives than do statements about matters of etiquette."[27] We may well feel that we have to act morally, and our moral convictions have a place in our lives that is especially important. To say that we feel we must do something as a matter of morality is not at all to say that we just happen to feel like it or that it just happens to be a social norm that this is what one does. Rather, it may be symptomatic of a conviction we feel powerfully, a commitment we do not waver in, perhaps reinforced by tradition and moral teaching.

But it is not enough to explain the force of the moral "should" in terms of the import of what we care about and the way in which it is learned. They are part of the account, but there is more to it. While morality may not involve an a priori rational command or irresistibility, it does involve confrontation, confrontation with the world that is the object of practical cognition. This is the sense in which there is inescapability. We can ignore the world, practically misconceive it, deceive ourselves about it, and so forth, but it is there nonetheless and remains ethically significant for practical reasoners. In many discussions of morality, explanations of what makes a principle or a consideration a moral one point to something about the agent—that he universalizes a rule, or that an imperative is regarded as a command, or that a decision is made. None of this, however, will tell us what morality is about and what moral claims properly answer to. The strategies just mentioned are often followed in order to get the necessary prescriptivity into morality, prescriptivity that no object or property possesses in itself. But practical understanding can provide the motivational dimension of morality, and what is at issue is what needs to be understood, not what is chosen or prescribed.

The understanding itself provides reasons for action, in that practical reasoning considers facts in terms of what is good to do. The "ought" of morality does not need to be imported from outside the comprehension, as something essentially distinct from it, as an independent desire or internalization of an enforced social norm. It would be incorrect to say that there is no role for desire or the passions here. Practical comprehension is for the sake of action, and desire is involved in that it concerns what is to be done. But it need not be an antecedent or independent desire, fully specifiable separately from judgment about what to do. Practical dispositions can be cognitively informed desires. What one does, one wants to do, but not always on account of a want distinct from or having motivational force separate from a judgment of what to do.

This account is similar to and, to some extent, indebted to the account McDowell gives in "Are Moral Requirements Hypothetical Imperatives?" In it, he says that "according to this position, then, a failure to see reason to act virtuously stems, not from the lack of a desire on which the rational influence of moral requirements is conditional, but from the lack of a distinctive way of seeing situations. If that perceptual capacity is possessed and exercised, it yields non-hypothetical reasons for acting."[28] There is a desire involved to the extent that to acknowledge a reason to act is to recognize a certain action as choiceworthy, but the desire need not be independent of and contingently engaged to the cognition of the facts. To understand things a certain way is simply to be in possession of reasons to act or to valuationally judge them in certain ways. In this respect, morality is not introduced into the world by subjects' appetition or sensibility; rather, it is a cognitively contentful response to the world, a response to a confrontation with facts that recognizes them as reasons. In order for there to be nonhypothetical moral requirements, all that is needed is a world that includes practical reasoners. Their practical cognition yields moral reasons. Respecting people basically amounts to actively attending to facts about them and their situations in order to achieve a right comprehension of what is ethically relevant.

In the same paper, McDowell notes that one difference between the genuinely virtuous person and the person who is weak is that "the virtuous person conceives the relevant sorts of situation in such a way that considerations which would otherwise be reasons for acting differently are silenced by the recognized requirement."[29] The virtuous person does not beat back inclinations to do other than what virtue requires; she doesn't renounce something else. Rather, she is insulated from the contrary-to-virtue inclinations in situations in which virtuous action is called for. And McDowell admits, without apology, that this "view of virtue obviously involves a high degree of idealization."[30] If one's virtues are perfect, there is not a conflict between obligation and inclination that is always settled in favor of the former. The person with complete virtue willingly does what virtue requires—willingly in the sense that, given her second nature, she appreciates a certain action as right and has no tendency to do otherwise. She enjoys acting well, and for a character like that, it is natural to act that way. The morally well ordered person recognizes certain kinds of considerations as constituting nonhypothetical moral reasons. Additionally, she is unmoved, or at least moved less, by the possibilities of appreciating the situation differently. For example, in stopping to assist someone whose vehicle is broken down, the good person does not simply consider, "What can I get from this guy if I help?" If the suggestion is made, perhaps because the person looks desperate or it is a very lightly traveled road and help from others is not likely to come soon, a morally sound individual will reject these considerations as either irrelevant or redescribe them as further considerations in favor of just helping without the motive of reward. Many exercises of what we recognize as virtue include a general disposition of respect for others, a general disposition to take ethical reasons as authoritative. If, given the nature of a kind (human beings), there are real goods for individuals of that kind, realizable through their own activity, then it is a form of respect for them to act so as to realize those goods and to enable them to do so. It is through attention to good that concern for others is expressed and actualized. This may entail renouncing or overcoming the influence of other motivations and ends, or it may be a settled disposition to conceive situations in such a way that the other influences simply do not operate.

What remains to be explained is how practical realism distinguishes between ethical practical reasoning and nonethical practical reasoning. Practical cognition is not exclusively moral, and the issue of what is distinctive about ethical cognition and reasoning is briefly taken up in the conclusion.

Conclusion

In the Introduction I said that the issue of distinguishing ethical from nonethical practical reasoning would have to be taken up. Something needs to be said about this because, according to practical realism, practical reasoning generally is a cognitive matter, in the sense that it is responsive to reality or, alternatively, reality is prescriptive for it. Prudential reasoning and productive reasoning must also respond to reality in order to be effective. They recognize situations or possibilities as supplying considerations that count as reasons. So, if practical reasoning in its various forms has the world as its object, how are we to mark off what counts as its ethical form?

REALISM AND PRACTICAL REASON

In what way is reality prescriptive for practical reasoning generally? Consider the tactics of some types of game playing, baseball, for example. It is a maxim of baseball strategy that it is a bad thing to walk the opposing team's lead-off batter. It creates too easy an opportunity for the opposition to score. This maxim only makes sense given that a certain game has been invented and is played a certain way. Nonetheless, given what the game consists in, to yield a walk, and in particular a walk to the lead-off hitter, is something the team in the field has very good reason not to do. The game is an artifact, and the goods appropriate to play and strategy are dependent upon its artifactual character. Still, given what the game is, certain realities of it are prescriptive for players and managers. The realities may change as the game evolves. Even if the rules of the game stay the same, the way it is played changes; consider the increasingly important role of relief pitchers and "bit players," who enter the game only in certain situations. The point is not that the realities of the game are fixed but that, whatever they are, they are prescriptive for players and managers. For that matter, they are prescriptive for sportswriters, too, since in order to do their job well, they need to understand the game. They are prescriptive in that judgments about what to do or to try to do are guided by the facts, however artifactual the reality.

We find a similar kind of prescriptivity in activities such as cooking. In order to prepare a certain food properly, steps must be taken in a specific order: some things need to be chilled, others beaten (but not too much, etc.), and the like. The recipes are inventions, perhaps accidental inventions. But practical cognition is active in making the dishes, and that is what distinguishes cooking (or at least much of it) from just getting something to eat or playing at cooking.

Examples of the realism of nonethical practical reason can be easily multiplied and found in all variety of contexts. Doing or making well is often a world-guided business. Once a certain reality "gets going," once it is artifactually or institutionally established, practical reasoning concerning it or within it is world-guided. If you want to raise hunting dogs rather than guard dogs, you need to know about breeding, training, exercise, and obedience. If you are an attorney involved in a certain type of suit, there are established procedures and protocols to conform to. If you want to irrigate for fruit trees rather than cereal grains, doing it successfully depends upon an understanding of natural and technical considerations.

These examples are readily interpreted as concerning institutional or artifactual goods, goods that are embedded in contexts of aims, interests, desires, and norms that are optional. The establishment and continued endorsement of these institutions is a matter of decision, and norms and rules are not grounded in or justified by the "nature of things." Morality is not an institution in the same sense. Moral requirements are justified by considerations that are objective in a way that institutional facts are not. Mackie, we saw, argued that basic notions of morality, such as obligation and universalization, are all properly explained in terms that do not refer to considerations of objective value. Obligation and universalization, he holds, are to be explained in terms of agents endorsing certain practices, kinds of reasons, and substantive practical principles. It is the special logic of morality, not general logic, that gives these life and force, and a person can opt out of that special logic or, presumably, just never go in for it in the first place. As a matter of fact (and one that Mackie is happy to accept), most people do endorse (imperfectly) the logic of obligation, moral reasons, and universalization. But that does not support a case for objectivity. There is nothing about the world "in itself" or logic as such that compels this. Morality, then, is an institutional matter, in his view.

What, then, according to realism is the mark of the ethical? We have rejected the explanation that there is a distinctive set of objects that ethical reasoning is uniquely concerned with. Another possibility is that morality is a system of imperatives tested by an a priori standard. But we have denied that morality is a system, that its requirements can be codified. We can accept that its requirements are categorical, but not for the Kantian reason that there is a single, fundamental formal criterion of moral validity *and* that it is a priori. For one thing, practical realism does not share Kant's starting point (at least in the *Foundations of the Metaphysics of Morals*), namely, the conflict between obligation and inclination. Practical realism does not interpret ethics primarily as an attempt to slay or securely chain the dragon of egoism or inclination. Kant's rational/empirical dualism generates a dualism of morality and egoism that is not part of this view. Moral theorizing and metaethical theorizing need not take as a starting point a clean break between the egoistic and the moral, or between self-concern and other-concern. Besides, maintaining that moral requirements are not inescapable and that the requirements of morality are hypothetically imperative is not a view logically tied to egoism. Philippa Foot,[1] for one, has made this clear, and it is clear in Mackie's view as well. Even in a theory that sharply distinguishes between the requirements of prudence and the requirements of morality, the former need not be interpreted in egoistic terms, much less hedonistic ones.

Numerous authors have remarked on the absence of a clean break between prudence and morality in Aristotle's view. He is interested in what it means to live a good life, and a sharp distinction between self-interest and concern for others is not an explanatorily significant part of his view. It is not that this sort of view does not give weight to other-concern. It does, but it does so as part of the project of explicating a good life, not as a separate or competing project. It is good to remember how much emphasis Aristotle puts on our being political animals, and that he maintains that the good of the community is superior to the good of an individual life. The kind of good life he prizes is a life in civil society, a life not possible outside it. In consequence, ethics is not a matter of moralizing prudence, where this is interpreted as self-interest. Human good is the focus of practical reasoning.

Our theory does not rely on Aristotle's teleology of human nature, at least not in exactly the form in which he develops it. Our focus is response to the ethical requirements found in the confrontation with reality, not the completion or perfection of a nature actualized through a life of rational activity (though features of the latter are elements of the former). But like Aristotle's view, ours has no place for a clean break between prudence and morality. This is not to say that they can never conflict but that the distinction does not rigidly map the terrain of argument and analysis.

Prudence and morality do not automatically put competing demands on us because leading a good life, doing well at the kind of life one has chosen, has among its conditions meeting ethical requirements. Acting from a concern for human goods, needs, and interests is part of a sound conception of a choiceworthy life. Someone whose purposes and goals, or manner of pursuing them, are indifferent to ethical considerations or despise or flout them is leading a life that practical reason can not credential. A correct understanding of one's own good and the characteristics needed to realize it includes an understanding of human good, not as a distinct and independent concern for others but as an appreciation of things that are general and that apply to oneself as well. If we think of ethical concern as an independent commitment, then we can find it problematic how to reconcile it with one's own good. But ethical concern is not an imposition on practical reasoning; it is ingredient in it when it is engaged with objective conceptions of good.

This is not to say that there is nothing that distinguishes the ethical from the nonethical. Any number of projects and practices are evidently nonethical. One can exercise sound or unsound practical reasoning in choosing how these things fit into a good life, but they do not have intrinsic ethical significance. We can judge certain actions or policies of action as reckless, advisable, unpromising, responsible, and so forth, without these being morally loaded in any particular way. But our conception of prudence is wider and richer than this, encompassing practical knowledge of human good, where there is nothing privileged or primary about self-interest. Ethical considerations are not just one possibility among the various things that can be regarded as important. They are recognized as important by sound practical reasoning, and it is not fully sound if the agent does not appreciate their importance. Aristotle's focus was not self-interest versus concern for others; it was the distinction between what is valuable or desirable for its own sake versus what is desirable for the sake of something else. It would not be quite right to say that Aristotle was not concerned with morality, that he was only concerned with something else, namely, what is a good life. Concern for morality is ingredient in this and not displaced or ignored by it. It would be odd to criticize for ignoring morality a theory of what it is for human beings to flourish and live well in political communities. If anything, this sort of approach narrows the distance between morality and concern for one's own good, implicating each in the other in fundamental ways. To act well is to act on an understanding of what is good or what it is good to do, where "good" is not essentially "good to *me*" but good to my being this kind of being. So, in acting from an understanding of good in this sense, there is not a general, structural problem of reconciling or relating self-concern with other-concern. I do not mean that the two simply coincide. But morality, in this view, is not mainly about how the interests or welfare of others restrict one's own interests. Rather, it concerns what is good for a kind of being, what is good for a *nature*.

It is the notion of the intrinsic worth of an action that is crucial to locating ethics in the geography of practical reason. Ethics has to do with action that realizes intrinsic value, and the judgment of this is cognitive. The phrase "action that realizes intrinsic value" cries out for explication. The claim is that practical reasoning can recognize features of situations that constitute categorical requirements on action. Practical reasoning is not all instrumental reasoning, either in the sense that it recognizes nothing to have intrinsic value or in the sense that what it recognizes as having it is something supplied from outside reason. For ethics, what is of primary importance about practical reason is not that reason can be instrumental but that it is *reason*, that action can be informed by a true conception of what to do. For a being with desires but without reason, there are no conceptions of intrinsic worth. There are goods for it, real goods. But its motion is not directed and evaluated by it under conceptions of intrinsic worth. Consideration, weighing, comparing, ordering, revising, and so forth—all those things we do concerning desires, plans, options for action are exercises of reason. And so is appreciating intrinsic worth.

Something has intrinsic worth for us because we have a nature to which desire and sensibility are essential, but they are not the arbiters of intrinsic worth.

The good that is realized in ethical responses to reality is not good that is conditional upon what people's desires happen to be. It is good appropriate to what a human being is. This is not because human beings have a particular function but because they have a nature. Given what they are, there are real goods for them, real needs and interests that they have, and ethical practical reasoning is reasoning that appreciates situations in terms of their significance for these. In this sense neither self-concern nor other-concern is straightforwardly primary or ethically privileged. Given our accounts of self-love and friendship, it should be plausible to see the two kinds of concern as substantially interconnected; good action promotes both, and they are each best promoted and served by ethically good action. The central questions of ethics are not properly motivated by the problem of how one is able, or required to take others into consideration. They are motivated by the issue of what has intrinsic worth for a being with this nature. And answers to this question will be based upon considerations of how desire can be informed by truth. If we do what is true, if we act on an understanding of good, then our action is a literal realization or actualization of good.

There are countless sortals under which someone can be judged to be good, bad, or indifferent, for example, as mayor, shopkeeper, parent, hunter, cook, and so on. Being a good parent is not just a biological notion; it involves being (in many ways) a good person. And similarly for being a good son or daughter. Being a good (or bad) cook is not like that. A terrible person can be a terrific cook. An ethically good person is not good on account of successfully realizing any specific function; he acts on an understanding of good not sortally restricted to a category. Whether one is a mayor, a bus driver, a medical technician, or a house cleaner, there is an understanding of good that is prescriptive for all of them. We do not know what restricted sortals will be true of our children, but we want them to be good people. This isn't a matter of their fulfilling a certain function. It is a matter of their coming to have a kind of practical knowledge that is general, in the sense that it is not restricted to any particular context of action or role. This is how the ethical virtues differ from other practical virtues. A situation judged in terms of ethical good is not judged primarily from the standpoint of any particular office or position one might have or in terms of the special concerns one has insofar as a restricted sortal applies to the agent.

Given one's position (as general, mother, court clerk, safety inspector) one has specific responsibilities that others do not have. What one needs to take into account as ethically significant can differ according to one's special roles and offices. But that conditionality does not mean that what is morally required is in any way conditional. The moral considerations are the same for everybody, but what considerations one most directly confronts differs according to sortal-restricted positions in a situation. The moral reasons there are to do x or refrain from it are the same for everybody as practical reasoners. What is required of a particular agent, however, may depend upon how she is placed in the situation or got into it. The differences in requirements are the result of what we might call institutional factors; but what is required as a matter of morality is not determined by institutional factors. The confrontation of common practical reason with the world yields moral requirements, though the angle of confrontation can make a difference to what practical reason and the world require. Tank crews, emergency room nurses, and political leaders all need to be courageous, but courage may well demand different things of them. The good that one properly answers to in the ethical exercise of practical reason is common across persons and not determined by their subjective commitments, interests, or roles. Responding to it is not just a skill developed as a special kind of expertise suited to this or that task, purpose, or role. The good that ethical reason is concerned with is not specialized, either in terms of whom it is good for or in terms of skills needed to recognize and realize it.

The capacity to recognize what is morally required is developed through learning and experience, but it is not a technical capacity, a capacity for making. (The capacities for throwing strikes in baseball and having soufflés come out well are capacities for making.) Ethical action is not a matter of φing well or ψing well but simply of acting well; it is not a matter of regarding the facts or situation essentially or primarily in terms of purposes or interests one has under a sortal other than *human being*.

Since our project is not to identify human good in terms of a function of human beings, the objection that there are many things distinctive of humans and thus we cannot tell which to use as a basis for ethics loses its force. Bernard Williams, for example, argues that

> if one approached without preconceptions the question of finding characteristics which differentiate men from other animals, one could as well, on these principles, end up with a morality which exhorted men to spend as much time as possible in making fire; or developing peculiarly human physical characteristics; or having sexual intercourse without regard to season; or despoiling the environment and upsetting the balance of nature; or killing things for fun.[2]

It is easy to abuse what Aristotle says about the *ergon* of a human being. His view is that because he is rational, a human being organizes his life in accord with conceptions of good and that a human being can only succeed in living a distinctively human life if he has correct conceptions of good. Activity guided by them brings a person and maintains a person in the natural (ideal) state for a human being. For the purposes of the realism defended here, this Aristotelian claim is apt. It is our rationality that enables us to appreciate ethical value, both in recognizing it and in enjoying acting from the understanding of it. While there are many things a human being can do that differentiate him from other kinds of things, it is not trivial or arbitrary to settle on reasoning as the crucial differentia of a human life. Reason has a function. It is a capacity for understanding. It has authority, in the sense that when it operates well, it minimizes the risk of error or ignorance; it has the authority of knowing the truth. In this respect we can say that because a human being is rational, his function is to act rationally. He has the capacity to lead his life in accord with conceptions of good and cannot live well without doing so. But this is still not to say that there is a human function, in the sense of something that a human is for. Moreover, it is easy to criticize the Aristotelian claim that rational activity is our function if we, in an un-Aristotelian way, cleanly break apart reason and desire from each other. If we do that, then we can more easily claim either that, whatever our ends are, they must come from desire or that we have many different impulses and desires, and reason cannot privilege one over another. But as we have argued, reason and desire are not two different powers in us that combine to yield action. Our desiring can be rational desiring and our reason is practical only because it is desiderative. Our characteristic activity is rational activity, since, given our nature, acting for an end is a rational business—not *purely* rational, whatever that might be claimed to mean, but also not the result of reason being connected up to something else nonrational. A practical reasoner does not apply reason to desire; a practical reasoner acts through desiderative reasoning.

Williams has also argued that even if there were one especially important piece of ethical knowledge, knowledge that a certain kind of life was best, there would still not be a systematic body of world-guided ethical knowledge. It is useful to consider his argument here, since our response to it will draw on many of the themes and theses so far developed.

REALISM AND REFLECTION

In *Ethics and the Limits of Philosophy* Williams denied the possibility of convergence in ethical knowledge resembling the possibility of convergence in scientific knowledge. His argument turns in part on the claim that reflection about scientific thought reveals that an "absolute conception" of how the world is *anyway* is what it can converge on but that there is no counterpart for ethical knowledge.[3] Moreover, whatever convergence there were to be in ethical thought would be a convergence of practical reason, a convergence socially brought about, by people thinking it good to have certain beliefs because of their dispositions and desires.[4] The convergence would not be a result of ethical truths explaining why people had the ethical conceptions they have; it would not be caused by ethical truth.[5] Moreover, there would, at the reflective level, be one piece of ethical knowledge, at most: that a certain kind of life was best.[6] There would not be a *system* of ethical knowledge organized by inferential and explanatory connections covering ethical matters in a rigorous, organized manner. This is partly true; ethical knowledge does not take the form of an overall, systematic theory of ethical matters in anything like the way physical theory does for physical matters. It need not, and it should not be expected to. For one thing, it is not a body of knowledge concerning an object or an order that is given in the same way the natural world-order is given for scientific knowledge. Its importance lies in its connection with what is to be done, what is to be actualized, as well as in ascertaining how things are.

One main reason Williams believes there cannot be much objective ethical knowledge is that, even if there were a best kind of life, the knowledge that this was so could not be based upon or derived from an absolute conception of human nature.[7] Such a conception in itself does not determine a unique specification of human well-being, and besides, the commitment to lead that kind of life would have its origin in dispositions and desires and not knowledge of it as a theoretical matter. This is the high-level reason, the reason at the level of reflective ascent, why ethical knowledge cannot be world-guided.

There is, though, one important affinity between scientific and ethical knowledge. Both depend upon certain kinds of concerns and dispositions. The seeking of either is motivated by a concern for truth. There is a way the world is anyway, and there may be a maximally perspective-independent conception of it that inquirers could converge upon. But the achievement of that absolute conception, or any approximation of it, requires a concern for truth or knowledge and that concern is a practical matter. Granted, a commitment to ethical life is not just another expression of exactly this same concern, and it involves different dispositions. But neither practical knowledge nor scientific knowledge is achievable without a sustained concern for truth—in the latter case to know it; in the former case to know it and act on it, to take it as a reason for the doing or actualization of something. A commitment to have one's conceptions guided by the world is a common condition of the scientific and the practical.

Still, one could insist that the justification of scientific knowledge claims is essentially different from the justification of ethical knowledge claims. The acceptance of ethical claims seems to depend upon noncognitive dispositions in a way that the acceptance of scientific claims does not. Recognizing that an ethical claim is true or is a piece of ethical knowledge depends upon the subject having certain concerns and conceptions of what is ethically important. It involves sensitivity to the significance of features of actions, characteristics, or situations. Ethical truth will not be recognized as such by persons who are unreceptive to it on account of their interests, dispositions, and experience. So, it seems justification of ethical knowledge claims cannot be spelled out in terms of what is so in a way analogous to how justification proceeds for nonethical knowledge claims.

This difference is easy to overstate. As I've indicated, the pursuit of scientific knowledge depends upon practical dispositions and forms of concern, and these figure no less in the articulation and acceptance of justifications. Acceptance and conviction with respect to knowledge claims are rational matters, but not matters of pure reason if that means there is no role in them for practical commitments and sensitivity. Persons can be unresponsive to or unreceptive to scientific considerations, and if this is overcome, it is not just because they have freed themselves of their irrational prejudices or other clutter but because their interest in the matter or in the truth is of the right sort. They *want* the truth and want to understand what makes a claim a true one. This is not a matter of eliminating interest but of reordering it.

In the ethical context, there is, in addition to the concern for truth, the concern to guide action by it motivated by appreciation of its importance.

Williams says that "reflection on the excellence of a life does not itself establish the truth of judgments using those concepts or of the agent's other ethical judgments. Instead it shows that there is good reason (granted the commitment to an ethical life) to live a life that involves those concepts and those beliefs."[8] He seems to be skeptical of the extent and systematic character of ethical knowledge because, as we reflectively ascend, our concepts become thinner and there is diminishing potential for world-guidedness. Furthermore, the ethical knowledge that we already possessed at the ground level will not be reinforced by reflective ascent. But Williams is overstating the extent to which ethical knowledge needs to resemble scientific knowledge. Scientific knowledge, as he describes it, could converge on an absolute conception. There is no reason to think that for it to be knowledge, ethical knowledge would have to converge on an absolute conception of value reality. For one thing, ethics may be realist, pluralist, and acknowledge incommensurable values. We do not close in on ethical truth by theoretical convergence in a way analogous to closing in on scientific truth. This is not because ethical truth is partial or fragmentary but because it concerns particulars, and often the particulars are actions to be done. And they may not all be justified by a single supertheory.

Ethical knowledge is knowledge of what is objectively good for human practical reasoners. This is not the perspective of a particular social world, but it is a perspective for a social world. A certain kind of social world is conducive to the development, persistence, and transmission of this perspective—for example, a social world in which there is ethical respect to a high degree and there are many exemplars of good. That it is social, that it is not there *anyway*, does not diminish the objectivity of the justification for what makes it a good one.

There may be no theoretical argument that would prove to any rational person that an ethical knowledge claim is true. For one thing, a person will only be able to fully understand what Williams calls ethical "reflection" if his practical reason is well ordered. So, one difference between the ethical comprehension of the world and the scientific comprehension of it is that reflection on the former yields knowledge of good achievable only through being good. In that respect, Williams may be right that reflection will not yield a conception of ethical requirements *and* lead the reflecting agent into the ethical life. But it does not follow from this that there are not objective truths or that there is no ethical knowledge at the level of reflective ascent. There is, but it is a dialectical ascent, with its starting points in the ethical goodness of the agent. It is not a consequence of a theoretical conception of human nature. It is practical knowledge of practical activity and dispositions and the consideration of the world as a setting for practical reasoning.

Persons with practical wisdom have something more than confidence in the rightness of their practical comprehension. They have knowledge of it. But it is not knowledge arrived at by systematic inquiry. It is consequent upon reflection on their conception of what is ethically important and upon their character. There is no direct route to ethical knowledge for reflection. It is a route that goes through their dispositions, judgments, and practices. They must have ethical commitments and concerns in order to have reflective ethical knowledge (which is not to say that there is not prereflective ethical knowledge). In the ethical context, the comprehension of the justification of knowledge claims depends upon an established capacity for good judgment. There is no general epistemology of ethical claims available both to those who nonaccidently have mostly true beliefs about ethical matters and to those who do not. A certain kind of starting point for justificatory reflection is needed. But for one who occupies that starting point, it can be seen that ethical truth is world-guided and that ethical description can truly express objective ethical significance.

It is not clear why Williams thinks it important that there should or should not be ethical knowledge at the level of reflective ascent and that it should explain or justify claims closer to ground level. Realism plainly does not require a comprehensive theory of, say, good or right, one into which all particular judgments are fitted. Realism, at least the sort defended here, takes as its focal concern the ethical significance of the specific features of concrete situations. Williams' undertaking—to find out if distinctively philosophical projects of reflection on practical reason or what it is to be a practical reasoner will both yield a specification of the ethical life and lead a person into that life—should not be identified with answering the question whether there are objective ethical truths. His question is a perfectly reasonable one, but it does not fix the agenda for inquiry concerning objectivity or realism. The issue is not that as we go up the ladder of generality, our ethical conceptions get thinner and are less world-guided and thus they cannot adequately justify and explain lower-level conceptions and judgments. Rather, the sort of reflective ascent that centrally concerns Williams is simply not an essential feature of ethical conception, justification, or explanation. Realism can live without it, though conceptions and explanations of increasing generality can be brought into view and are valuable. Realist concern is with what is actually confronted in the world, not with deriving what to do from the top down in a theoretical structure.

I have remarked that having the sorts of dispositions of sensibility and desire that enable a person to judge correctly precedes a discursive understanding of what makes for correct judgment. As McDowell stated in "Are Moral Requirements Hypothetical Imperatives?":

> It would be wrong to infer that the conceptions of situations which constitute the reasons are available equally to people who are not swayed by them, and weigh with those who are swayed only contingently upon their possession of an independent desire. . . . We should say that the relevant conceptions are not so much as possessed except by those whose wills are influenced appropriately. Their status as reasons is hypothetical only in this truistic sense: they sway only those who *have* them.[9]

Having practical comprehension that gets ethical significance right requires cognitive dispositions. These are not cognitive dispositions connected up with independent desires or feelings. Being practically well ordered, having ethical virtue, is a matter of a desiring, feeling agent having abilities to recognize, judge, and choose where the ordering of desire and feeling is a feature of practical cognition. It enables the agent to recognize reasons that are reasons for action, because the agent is a being with concerns and interests that she would lack were she not an essentially desiring being. But the recognition of situations and facts as constituting reasons is a cognitive recognition. It is not made by a separate faculty of intuition. And for the agent who makes such recognitions, the reasons are categorical reasons for actions.

Ethical judgment, then, is both cognitive and world-guided; the excellences of the agent that are needed for it are excellences of rational capacities. Ethical significance is not neutrally disclosed to all alike, some having the desire to act on it, others not. It is disclosed only to agents of certain kinds, but what is disclosed is objective. The acknowledgment of *this* fact is a result of reflection. Reflection can justify and illuminate ethical claims, but it needs to be reflection that is already apt to disclose truths because it has the right starting points. On the other hand, it is not a shortcoming of reflection that it does not yield a truth-by-truth, principle-by-principle, systematic conception of ethics.

Ethical reflection does not initially take as its object anything so broad as human nature or the best kind of life. It progresses toward generalizations rather than working down from high-level principles to more specific pieces of ethical knowledge. The practically wise individual can come to understand the truth of generalizations or principles because he has good judgment concerning particulars. Nor does ethical knowledge come apart at the reflective level because it does not achieve a conception of a uniquely best kind of life for an individual or a society. That there should be such a thing is not a condition of ethical knowledge. The fact that there is not some totalizing conception of good or right that is instantiated in each case is not a problem for realist objectivity.

Granted I have been using *good* as a generic term in this book, a term to refer to what ethical reasoning is concerned with. But there is the good of friendship, of generosity, of justice, of redressing wrong, of minimizing harm, of patience, and so on, and the good of each is a matter of the realities of specific situations. That ethical good is real is not to say that there is just one thing that constitutes it. There is not an analytic taxonomy of good, a procedure of conceptual elaboration of it independent of the concrete contingents in which it is found or realizable. Attention to and concern with ethical good is not attention to and concern with just one thing expressible by one value-concept.[10]

FINIS

In the chapters on moral psychology, we examined the role of ethical practical reasoning in the realization of good for the individual, its realization in sustained relations between persons with knowledge of each other, and in relations with and attitudes toward people in general, even where there is no special concern for them as *those* individuals. Self-love, friendship, and respect share normative bases. Sound practical reasoning, including both correct understanding and action guided by it, is the core of all three, which is to say that it is the core of the most important relations humans have and enter into. Ethical practical reasoning is not a special type of practical reasoning, or a kind of control on nonethical practical reasoning. There is no distinctive context or end or principle that marks it off. It is, rather, the culmination of our capacity for practical reasoning, a kind of completion or perfection of it, in that it is that by which agents appreciate and act on objective considerations of intrinsic value.

Being moral is a way of responding, through action, to a right understanding of the world. What is good for human beings ideally does not figure in motivation as a kind of principled constraint, taking the form of an imperative at odds with other tendencies to act. In a person with sound judgment and sound character, it is normal and natural to respond to the recognition of intrinsic value with action. McDowell makes a similar point in presenting his own position: "according to this position, then, a failure to see reason to act virtuously stems, not from the lack of a desire on which the rational influence of moral requirements is conditional, but from the lack of a distinctive way of seeing situations."[11] He puts the weight of his argument on the notion of a perceptual capacity, a way of seeing situations that yields reasons not conditional upon independent desires. There is desire, a want to do the action, in the sense that the agent recognizes decisive reasons insofar as the recognition, the "distinctive way of seeing" the situation, includes motivational dispositions. That is, one's orientation toward ends in acting includes habits of wanting to do what is intrinsically good (which is not the same as an antecedent occurrent inclination or desire, or a coincident one). The claim of practical realism is that practical reason is a capacity for understanding the world, and this understanding can be prescriptive. We can attribute desires to people on the basis of what they recognize to be prescriptive. We can say with Aristotle that in the sound individual, desire is in agreement with what reason understands and that the intellect does not move us without desire. But desires that figure in morally sound action are not independent of practical cognition. They are the desires of one who understands correctly. A person can be said to have a general desire to act well, and the having of that desire is consequent upon the right understanding of what it is good to do. There are things that are categorically good for human beings to do; good for them not because they happen to want this or that but because they are capable of recognizing considerations of intrinsic value. When they respond to the world in this way, they are reasoning ethically.

Notes & References

TO THE PREFACE

1. Suppose there were a divine being but no finite, creaturely practical reasoners. Would there be ethical truth, ethical content to the world? There would still be value (what God saw that He had made would still be good), but there would not be ethical value without practical reasoners. For the world would not count for anything with respect to action and the realization of value by agents that deliberate and choose.

2. Mark Platts, *Ways of Meaning,* Routledge & Kegan Paul, London, 1979, p. 258.

TO THE INTRODUCTION

1. Sabina Lovibond, *Realism & Imagination In Ethics,* University of Minnesota Press, Minneapolis, 1983, p. 42.

2. Ibid., p. 43.

3. See Thomas Nagel, *The Possibility of Altruism,* Oxford University Press, Oxford, 1970. Alan Donagan, *The Theory of Morality,* University of Chicago Press, Chicago, 1977.

4. See J. L. Mackie, *Ethics: Inventing Right and Wrong,* Penguin, Harmondsworth, England, 1977; Gilbert Harman, *The Nature of Morality,* Oxford University Press, Oxford, 1979; Bernard Williams, *Ethics and the Limits of Philosophy,* Harvard University Press, Cambridge, 1985.

5. Simon Blackburn, "Errors and the Phenomenology of Value" in *Essays in Quasi-Realism,* Oxford University Press, New York, 1993, p. 157.

6. Immanuel Kant, *Critique of Practical Reason,* ed. L. W. Beck, Bobbs-Merrill, Indianapolis, 1956, p. 122.

7. Lewis White Beck, *A Commentary on Kant's Critique of Practical Reason,* University of Chicago Press, Chicago, 1960, p. 229.

8. Immanuel Kant, *Doctrine of Virtue,* trans. Mary Gregor, Harper & Row, New York, 1964, p. 99.

TO CHAPTER 1

1. J. L. Mackie, *Ethics: Inventing Right and Wrong,* Penguin, Harmondsworth, England, 1977, p. 35.

2. Ibid., p. 38.

3. Ibid., p. 49.

4. This, too, is an Aristotelian point, one that does not presuppose the sharp distinction between the cognitive and the affective, or the rational and the nonrational, that has been so prevalent in modern moral philosophy.

5. See John McDowell, "Values and Secondary Qualities" in *Essays on Moral Realism,* ed. Geoffrey Sayre-McCord, Cornell University Press, Ithaca, 1988. McDowell answers the question as follows: "Is there any alternative to thinking of it as capable of being captured, at least in theory, by a set of principles for superimposing values onto a value-free reality? The upshot is that the search for an evaluative outlook that one can endorse as rational becomes, virtually irresistibly, a search for a set of principles: a search for a *theory* of beauty or goodness" (pp. 179–180).

McDowell, for reasons similar to mine, rejects the claim that morality must be capturable and expressible as a theory.

6. B. Williams, *Ethics and the Limits of Philosophy,* Harvard University Press, Cambridge, 1985, p. 52.

7. Aristotle himself seems to have recognized incommensurability insofar as he does not definitely settle the issue of which is the best kind of life. Whether it is the active life or the contemplative life, the goods of the other remain real goods and are desirable for their own sake. Even if it is objected that the character of Aristotle's project requires him to settle on a uniquely best kind of life, his ethical inquiry and reflection indicate a way in which objective goods grounded in human rational nature can be ethically central, though the question of a human function is not resolved.

8. Nicholas Sturgeon uses the case of Hitler's depravity to criticize Harman's argument that moral facts are explanatorily irrelevant in accounting for moral observations. Sturgeon's version of realism is different in some ways from mine, but his realist objections to Harman's view are congenial in several respects to this account. Our judgment that Hitler was depraved is a factual one, and Hitler's being depraved is part of the explanation of what he did and part of the explanation for our observing that he is depraved. See "Moral Explanations" in *Essays on Moral Realism,* ed. G. Sayre-McCord, Cornell University Press, Ithaca, 1988.

9. Mackie, *Ethics: Inventing Right and Wrong,* Penguin, Harmondsworth, England, 1977, p. 38.

10. David Brink, *Moral Realism and the Foundations of Ethics,* Cambridge University Press, New York, 1989, p. 175.

11. Nicholas Sturgeon, "Harman on Moral Explanations of Natural Facts" in Norman Gillespie, *Spindel Conference 1986: Moral Realism, Southern Journal of Philosophy,* supp. vol. 24, p. 75.

12. Mark Platts uses this notion of the nonmoral "fixing" the moral in *Ways of Meaning,* Routledge & Kegan Paul, London, 1979.

13. Simon Blackburn, "Moral Realism" in *Essays in Quasi-Realism,* Oxford University Press, New York, 1993, p. 122.

14. Ibid., p. 123.

15. Ibid., p. 129.

16. Simon Blackburn, "How to Be an Ethical Antirealist" in *Midwest Studies in Philosophy*, ed. Peter French, Theodore Uehling, Jr. and Howard Wettstein, University of Minnesota Press, Minneapolis, 1988, p. 367.

17. Simon Blackburn, *Spreading the Word*, Oxford University Press, Oxford, 1984, p. 169.

18. Ibid., p. 171.

19. Ibid.

20. Ibid.

21. Ibid.

22. Ibid., p. 184.

23. Ibid., p. 186.

24. Mackie, *Ethics: Inventing Right and Wrong*, p. 41.

25. Ibid., p. 33.

26. This sort of approach is defended in Brink, *Moral Realism and the Foundations of Ethics*. See especially chapter 6.

27. Ibid., p. 166.

28. Roderick Chisholm, "The Problem of the Criterion" in *The Foundations of Knowing*, University of Minnesota Press, Minneapolis, 1982; see pp. 65–69.

29. See, for example, Hume; also Bernard Williams, "Internal and External Reasons" in *Moral Luck*, Cambridge University Press, Cambridge, Mass., 1981; and *Ethics and the Limits of Philosophy*, Harvard University Press, Cambridge, 1985, especially chap. 3 and 8. See also Christine Korsgaard, "Skepticism about Practical Reason," *The Journal of Philosophy*, vol. 83, no. 1, 1986, pp. 5–25.

30. See Hilary Putnam, "Why There Isn't a Ready Made World" in *Realism and Reason*, Cambridge University Press, New York, 1983.

31. Ibid., pp. 215–216.

32. The presentation of these claims is obviously very compressed. I develop them more fully in "Representation, Cognition, and Realism" forthcoming in *The Journal of Speculative Philosophy*. In the article I argue that resources from Aristotle's philosophy of mind and metaphysics can be constructively integrated into the contemporary realist-antirealist debate, and that these resources can be important to the defense of realism. I discuss a non-representational theory of cognition, the causal theory of reference and causal realism. Much of the argument turns on the claim that there is nothing for cognition to be unless there is a mind-independent world to which it is a cognitive response, by being a conceptual realization of its intelligible features. See also John Haldane's "Mind-World Identity Theory and the Anti-Realist Challenge" in *Reality, Representation and Projection*, ed. by J. Haldane and C. Wright, Oxford University Press, New York, 1993, pp. 15–37.

33. H. Putnam, *Reason, Truth, and History*, Cambridge University Press, Cambridge, 1981, p. 54.

34. Ibid.

35. See chap. 2 of Putnam, *Reason, Truth, and History*; and especially "Models and reality" in *Realism and Reason*, vol. 3.

36. Michael Dummett, *Truth and Other Enigmas*, Harvard University Press, Cambridge, 1978, p. 358.

37. Nicholas Wolterstorff, "Realism vs. Anti-Realism" in *Proceedings and Addresses of the American Catholic Philosophical Association*, vol. 59, ed. D. O. Dahlstrom, American Catholic Philosophical Association, Washington, D.C., 1984, pp. 189–90.

38. Lawrence Bonjour, *The Structure of Empirical Knowledge*, Harvard University Press, Cambridge, 1985, p. 161.

39. This is one of the main points in William Alston, "Yes, Virginia, There is a Real World" in *Proceedings and Addresses of the American Philosophical Association*, vol. 52, no. 6, 1979, pp. 779–808. He argues in section 2 of this article (originally an APA Presidential Address) that

> from a realist point of view, epistemic justification is intimately connected with truth; not necessarily so closely connected that justification entails truth, but at least so closely connected that justification entails a considerable probability of truth. An epistemic principle that laid down sufficient conditions of justification such that we could know that a statement satisfied them while having no reason to think it true, would *ipso facto* be unacceptable.

In this article Alston also argues for the unavoidability of realism if we are to preserve reference and a tenable theory of what is involved in statement making.

40. David Wiggins, "A Sensible Subjectivism?" in *Needs, Values, Truth*, Blackwell, Oxford, 1991, p. 199.

41. Ibid., p. 197.

42. Ibid., p. 205.

43. Ibid., p. 209.

44. Blackburn, "How to be an Ehical Antirealist," p. 366.

45. Ibid., p. 208.

46. Ibid., p. 202.

47. Ibid.

48. This discussion of disclosure borrows heavily from chap. 2 of James F. Ross, *Introduction to the Philosophy of Religion*, Macmillan, Toronto, 1969.

49. John McDowell says that in trying to bring someone to see how circumstances constitute a reason for action, we back up the injunction "See it like this" with "helpful juxtapositions of cases, descriptions with carefully chosen terms and carefully placed emphasis and the like." The fact that there is no guarantee that we will succeed and that this is not straightforward evidence of the audience being irrational does not show that the appeal is an appeal to passion and not to reason. We may fail because we are not adequately skilled at this sort of work or because the audience, on account of their character, are not receptive to the appeal. But a change of conception and motivational disposition on their part is a change in cognitive state. See McDowell's discussion in "Are Moral Requirements Hypothetical Imperatives?" in *Proceedings of the Aristotelian Society*, supp. vol. 52, Compton Press, Tisbury, England, 1978, pp. 21–22.

50. Blackburn discusses whether a second-order error-theory does or should lead to revision of first-order practice and belief in "Errors and the Phenomenology of Value" in *Essays in Quasi-Realism*.

TO CHAPTER 2

1. See L. A. Kosman, "Being Properly Affected: Virtues and Feelings in Aristotle's Ethics" in *Essays on Aristotle's Ethics*, ed. Amelie Rorty, University of California Press, Berkeley and Los Angeles, 1980.

2. Bernard Williams, for example, writes: "Aristotle should not have believed that in the most basic respects, at least, people were responsible for their characters. He gives an account of moral development in terms of habituation and internalization that leaves little room for practical reason to alter radically the objectives that a grownup person has acquired." *Ethics and the Limits of Philosophy*, Harvard University Press, Cambridge, 1985, p. 39.

3. Richard Sorabji, "Involuntariness and Equity" in *Necessity, Cause, and Blame: Perspectives on Aristotle's Theory*, Cornell University Press, Ithaca, 1980, p. 168.

4. C. A. Campbell, *On Selfhood and Godhood*, George Allen and Unwin, New York, 1957, p. 177.

5. Ibid.

6. This part of the discussion is obviously influenced by John McDowell's "Virtue and Reason," *The Monist*, vol. 62, July 1979.

TO CHAPTER 3

1. Julia Annas, "Aristotle on Pleasure and Goodness" in *Essays on Aristotle's Ethics*, ed. Amelie Rorty, University of California Press, Berkeley and Los Angeles, 1980, p. 289.

2. Ibid., p. 290.

3. Immanuel Kant, *Lectures on Ethics*, trans. L. Infield, Hackett, Indianapolis, 1979, p. 215.

4. Ibid., p. 216.

5. Thomas Nagel, *The Possibility of Altruism*, Oxford University Press, Oxford, 1970, p. 42.

6. Ibid., p. 69.

7. Joseph Raz, *The Morality of Freedom*, Oxford University Press, Oxford, 1986, pp. 295–296.

8. Ibid., p. 289.

9. Ibid., p. 297.

TO CHAPTER 4

1. Humans are social beings not just in the sense that many of their activities are cooperative and that they in general seek and enjoy human company but also in the sense that the capacities for a distinctively human life are only developed in a social setting. Enquiry, production, the arts, and even the development of emotions and self-conceptions all require social life. What we understand as humor, despair, joy, friendship, fear, and a host of feelings, activities, and attitudes are not brought to social life but only develop and have what significance they have in social life.

2. In the *Politics* Aristotle says: "Hence arise in cities family connexions, brotherhoods, common sacrifices, amusements which draw men together. But these are created by friendship, for the will to live together is friendship" (1280b 36–38).

3. The sort of person an egoist might feel most admiration for and regard as best living up to egoist principles is likely to be just the sort of person an egoist could not be good friends with.

4. Sarah Broadie, *Ethics with Aristotle*, Oxford University Press, New York, 1991, p. 60.

5. My discussion of these issues borrows from John Cooper, "Aristotle on Friendship" in *Essays on Aristotle's Ethics*, ed. Amelie Rorty, University of California Press, Berkeley and Los Angeles, 1980, pp. 301–340.

6. Ibid., p. 322.

7. Frank Knight, "The Ethics of Competition," *The Quarterly Journal of Economics*, vol. 37, 1923, pp. 612–13.

8. Ibid., p. 612.

9. See, for example, Cooper, "Aristotle on Friendship," and Alan W. Price, *Love and Friendship in Plato and Aristotle*, Oxford University Press, New York, 1989, especially chap. 4.

10. Alan W. Price, *Love and Friendship*, p. 106.

11. In his discussion of those to whom we have friendly feelings, Aristotle in the *Rhetoric* includes "those who do not reproach us with what we have done amiss to them or they have done to help us, for both actions show a tendency to criticize us. And towards those who do not nurse grudges or store up grievances, but are always ready to make friends again" (1381b 3–5).

12. Kant, *Lectures on Ethics*, trans. L. Infield, Hackett, Indianapolis, 1979, p. 207.

13. Lawrence Blum, *Friendship, Altruism, and Morality*, Routledge & Kegan Paul, London, 1980, p. 64.

14. Ibid.

15. Ibid., p. 65.

16. Price, *Love and Friendship*, p. 106.

17. Blum, *Friendship, Altruism, and Morality*, p. 82.

TO CHAPTER 5

1. Sabina Lovibond, *Realism and Imagination in Ethics*, University of Minnesota Press, Minneapolis, 1983, p. 65.

2. Ibid., p. 63.

3. Iris Murdoch, *The Sovereignty of Good*, Routledge & Kegan Paul, London, 1970, p. 34.

4. Ibid., p. 41.

5. Ibid., p. 43.

6. Ibid., p. 75.
7. Ibid., p. 69.

TO CHAPTER 6

1. Bernard Williams, *Morality: An Introduction to Ethics*, Harper & Row, New York, 1972, p. 11.
2. Ibid.
3. J. L. Mackie, *Ethics: Inventing Right and Wrong*, Penguin, Harmondsworth, England, 1977, p. 98.
4. Immanuel Kant, *Foundations of the Metaphysics of Morals*, trans. Lewis W. Beck, Bobbs-Merrill, Indianapolis, 1959, p. 46.
5. Alan Donagan, *The Theory of Morality*, University of Chicago Press, Chicago, 1977, p. 233.
6. Kant, *Foundations of the Metaphysics of Morals*, p. 29.
7. Thomas Nagel, *The Possibility of Altruism*, Oxford University Press, Oxford, 1970, p. 116.
8. Ibid., p. 119.
9. Ibid., p. 142.
10. Ibid.
11. Alan Donagan, *The Theory of Morality*, Chicago, 1977, p. 237.
12. Ibid.
13. John McDowell, "Virtue and Reason," *The Monist*, vol. 62, July 1979, p. 336.
14. David Wiggins, "Universalizability, Impartiality, Truth" in *Needs, Value, Truth*, Blackwell, Oxford, 1987, p. 79.
15. Ibid.
16. Thomas Nagel, *The Possibility of Altruism*, p. 100.
17. Ibid., p. 108.
18. Iris Murdoch, *The Sovereignty of Good*, Routledge & Kegan Paul, London, 1970, p. 52.
19. Ibid., p. 103.
20. Ibid., p. 95.
21. J. L. Mackie, *Ethics: Inventing Right and Wrong*, p. 97.
22. Ibid., p. 93.
23. Ibid., p. 102.
24. Gilbert Harman, *The Nature of Morality*, Oxford University Press, New York, 1977, pp. 131–132.
25. Ibid., p. 106.
26. Philippa Foot, "Morality As a System of Hypothetical Imperatives" in *Virtues and Vices*, University of California Press, Berkeley and Los Angeles, 1978, p. 162.
27. Ibid., p. 164.
28. John McDowell, "Are Moral Requirements Hypothetical Imperatives?" in *Proceedings of the Aristotelian Society*, supp. vol. 52, Compton Press, Tisbury, England, 1978, p. 23.

29. Ibid., p. 28.
30. Ibid.

TO THE CONCLUSION

1. Philippa Foot, "Morality As a System of Hypothetical Imperatives" in *Virtues and Vices*, University of California Press, Berkeley and Los Angeles, 1978. See especially pp. 164–65.
2. Bernard Williams, *Morality: An Introduction to Ethics*, Harper & Row, New York, 1972, p. 64.
3. Bernard Williams, *Ethics and the Limits of Philosophy*, Harvard University Press, Cambridge, 1985, p. 139.
4. Ibid., p. 154.
5. Ibid., pp. 151–152.
6. Ibid., p. 154.
7. Ibid.
8. Ibid.
9. John McDowell, "Are Moral Requirements *Hypothetical Imperatives*?" in *Proceedings of The Aristotelian Society*, supp. vol. 52, Compton Press, Tisbury, England, 1978, p. 23.
10. In discussing realist pluralism, Robert Arrington writes that realist pluralists "reject the view that there is a common denominator to all moral values, a highest genus, and that specific moral features are determinants of this 'supervalue.' Far from the diverse moral properties being gradations of The Good or The Right, so that they may be weighed on a common scale and a determination made of which takes precedence, they may in fact be quite incommensurable." Robert L. Arrington, *Rationalism, Realism, and Relativism*, Cornell University Press, Ithaca, 1989, pp. 140–141.
11. McDowell, "Are Moral Requirements Hypothetical Imperatives?" p. 23.

Index

www.ingramcontent.com/pod-product-compliance
Lightning Source LLC
LaVergne TN
LVHW010347080826
844660LV00003B/218
9780878405831